DK First

FRENCH

Picture Dictionary

Contents

LONDON, NEW YORK, MUNICH,
MELBOURNE, and DELHI

Project Editor Anna Harrison
Editor Elise See Tai
Project Art Editors
Ann Cannings, Emy Manby
DTP Designer David McDonald
Production Harriet Maxwell
Translator Chantal Lamarque
with Elise Bradbury

Managing Editor
Scarlett O'Hara

First published in Great Britain in 2005 by
Dorling Kindersley Limited
80 Strand, London WC2R 0RL

A Penguin Company

2468109753

Copyright ©2005 Dorling Kindersley Limited

A catalogue record for this book is available
from the British Library.

ISBN 1 4053 1121 5

Colour reproduction by Colourscan, Singapore
Printed and bound in China by SNP Leefung

Discover more at
www.dk.com

How to use this dictionary

Find out how you can get the most from your dictionary. At the beginning of the book there are Topic pages. These include lots of useful words on a particular subject, such as *Pets* and *In the Park*. Each word has its translation and help on how to pronounce it. The words on the Topic pages can be found in the English A–Z and in the French A–Z. There are lots of other useful words here too. The verbs are in another section. At the back of the book there is a list of useful phrases for you to use when you practise your French with your friends.

Topic pages

topic heading

French entry word

French pronunciation

English translation

extra words on this subject

interesting fact

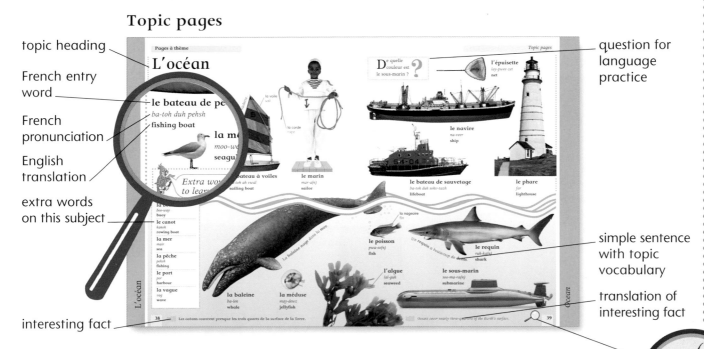

question for language practice

simple sentence with topic vocabulary

translation of interesting fact

English to French A–Z

first word on the page with the French translation

English entry word

French translation

often (adv)

French pronunciation

Look for me on the topic pages!

last word on the page with the French translation

this shows the first letter of the words on the page

Tout à mon sujet

All about me

Je suis **grande**.

la sœur
suhr
sister

le frère
frair
brother

le père
pair
father

la mère
mair
mother

le bébé
bay-bay
baby

Voici ma famille.

le grand-père
grandfather

la grand-mère
grandmother

les grands-parents
grah(n)-par-ah(n)
grandparents

l'enfant
lahn-fah(n)
child

la tante
tahnt
aunt

l'oncle
lonk-luh
uncle

Nous sommes **contentes** !

contente
kon-tahnt
happy

Thomas est **en colère**.

en colère
ah(n) ko-lehr
angry

Il y a environ 206 os dans ton corps !

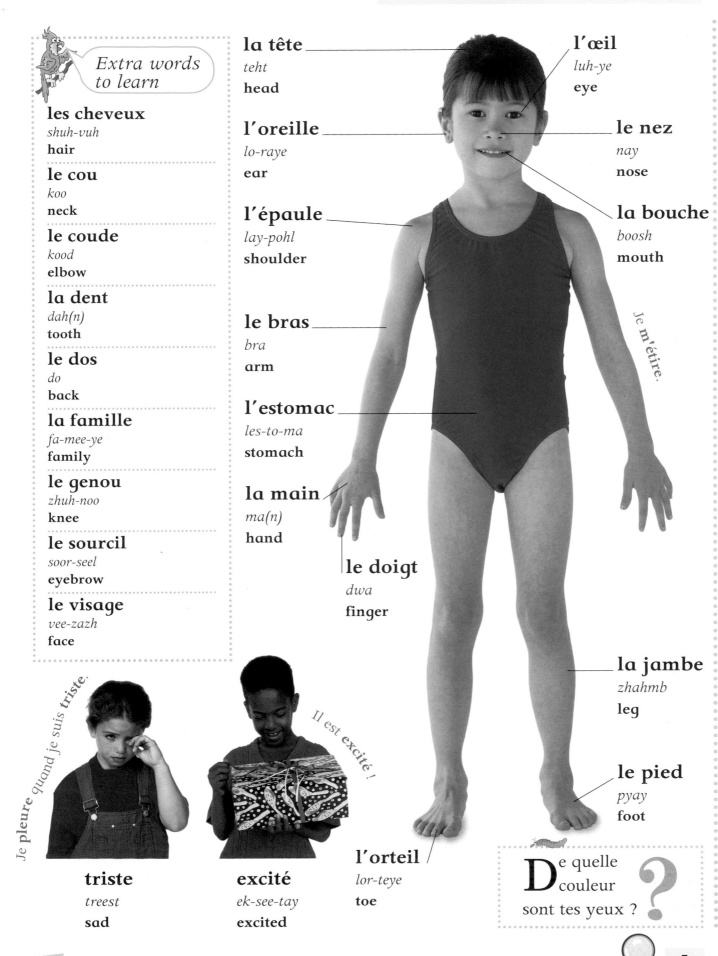

Extra words to learn

les cheveux
shuh-vuh
hair

le cou
koo
neck

le coude
kood
elbow

la dent
dah(n)
tooth

le dos
do
back

la famille
fa-mee-ye
family

le genou
zhuh-noo
knee

le sourcil
soor-seel
eyebrow

le visage
vee-zazh
face

la tête
teht
head

l'oreille
lo-raye
ear

l'épaule
lay-pohl
shoulder

le bras
bra
arm

l'estomac
les-to-ma
stomach

la main
ma(n)
hand

le doigt
dwa
finger

l'œil
luh-ye
eye

le nez
nay
nose

la bouche
boosh
mouth

Je m'étire.

la jambe
zhahmb
leg

le pied
pyay
foot

l'orteil
lor-teye
toe

Je pleure quand je suis triste.

triste
treest
sad

Il est excité !

excité
ek-see-tay
excited

De quelle couleur sont tes yeux **?**

There are about 206 bones in your body!

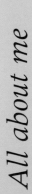

5

Les vêtements
Clothes

le bouton
button

les chaussettes

shoh-sets

socks

la chemise

shuh-meez

shirt

la fermeture
éclair
zip

la manche
sleeve

le jean

jeen

jeans

la poche
pocket

la polaire

po-lair

fleece

Mon manteau me tient chaud.

l'écharpe

lay-sharp

scarf

le gant
glove

les baskets

bas-ket

trainers

le manteau

mahn-toh

coat

**Extra words
to learn**

la chaussure

shoh-soor

shoe

le gant

gah(n)

glove

les lunettes

lew-net

glasses

la pantoufle

pahn-too-fluh

slipper

le pull-over

pewl-o-vair

jumper

le pyjama

pee-zha-ma

pyjamas

la robe

rob

dress

les sous-vêtements

soo-veht-mah(n)

underwear

Les jeans existent depuis plus de 130 ans !

la ceinture
belt

le pantalon
pahn-ta-lo(n)
trousers

le tee-shirt
tee-shirt
T-shirt

le short
short
shorts

le maillot de bain
ma-yoh duh ba(n)
swimsuit

la capuche
hood

la jupe
zhewp
skirt

le blouson
bloo-zo(n)
jacket

l'imperméable
lam-pair-may-a-bluh
raincoat

le jean
jeans

Les jeans et les baskets sont mes vêtements préférés.

les bottes
bot
boots

Aimes-tu **porter** des baskets **?**

Jeans are more than 130 years old!

Clothes

La cuisine
Kitchen

la casserole
saucepan

la poêle
pwal
frying pan

l'assiette
la-syet
plate

le four
oven

la cuisinière
kwee-zeen-yair
cooker

la cuillère
kwee-yehr
spoon

la tasse
tahss
mug

le livre
book

le torchon
tor-sho(n)
tea towel

la casserole
kass-rol
saucepan

Q u'y a-t-il dans la cuillère ?

La première cuisinière à gaz a été fabriquée en 1826.

Merci de **laver la vaisselle**.

le placard
cupboard

l'évier

layv-yay

sink

le congélateur
freezer

Extra words to learn

la bouilloire
booy-wahr
kettle

la cruche
krewsh
jug

le fer à repasser
fair ah ruh-pah-say
iron

le grille-pain
gree-ye-pa(n)
toaster

la machine à laver
ma-sheen ah la-vay
washing machine

le plateau
pla-toh
tray

la poubelle
poo-bell
bin

la tasse
tahss
cup

le couteau
koo-toh
knife

la fourchette
foor-shet
fork

le tablier
tab-lee-yay
apron

le gant de cuisine
gah(n) duh kwee-zeen
oven glove

le verre
vair
glass

le réfrigérateur
ray-free-zhair-a-tuhr
fridge

Aimes-tu faire de la pâtisserie ?

The first gas cooker was made in 1826.

Kitchen

La salle de bains
Bathroom

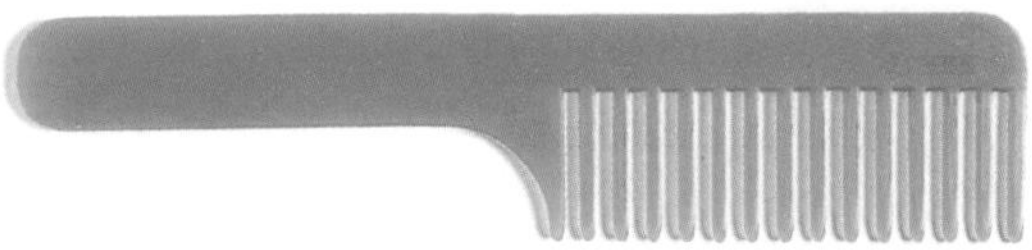

le peigne
pain-ye
comb

la baignoire
bayn-wahr
bath

C'est rigolo de faire des bulles.

le jouet
zhoo-way
toy

l'eau
loh
water

Je mets du dentifrice sur ma brosse à dents.

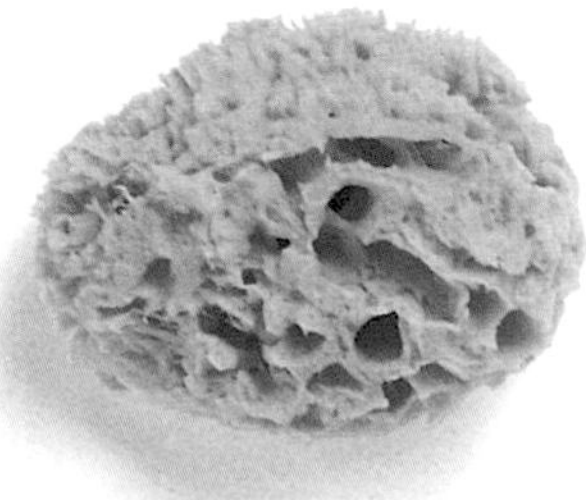

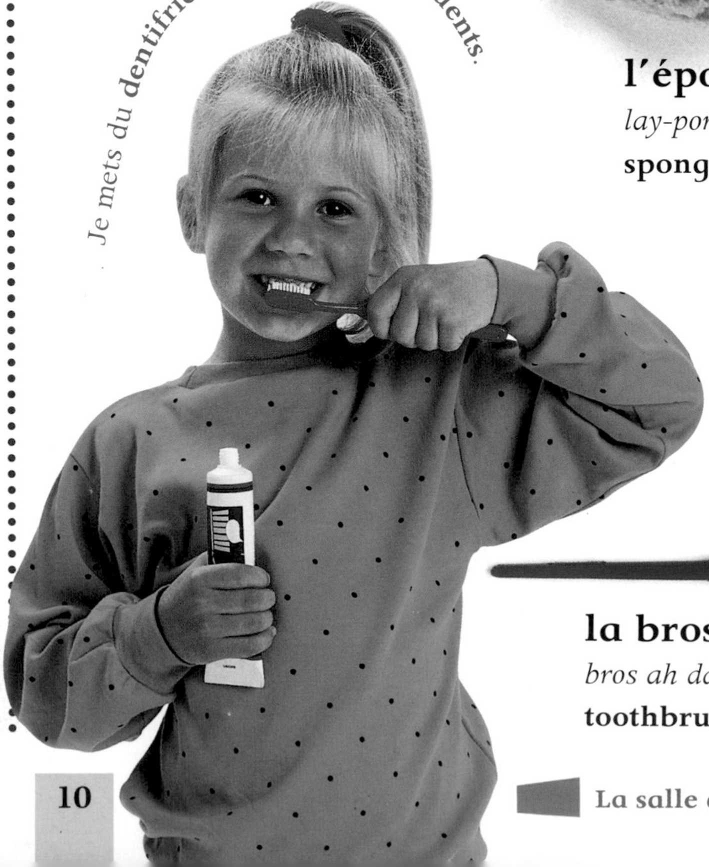

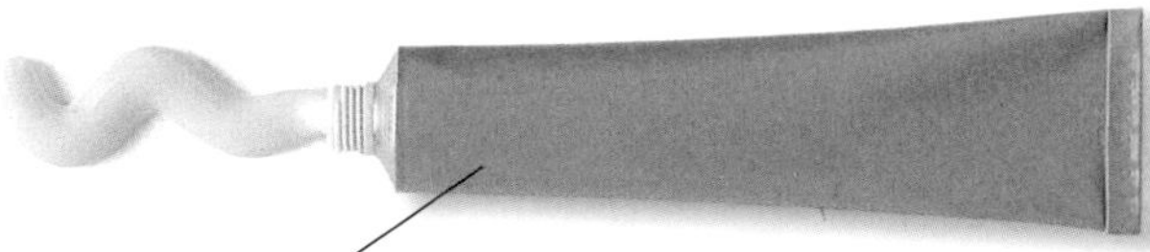

l'éponge
lay-ponzh
sponge

les serviettes
sair-vee-et
towels

le tube
tube

le dentifrice
dahn-tee-freess
toothpaste

la brosse à dents
bros ah dah(n)
toothbrush

Combien d'objets jaunes y a-t-il sur cette page ?

La salle de bains la plus chère a des toilettes en or !

le shampooing
shahm-pwa(n)
shampoo

le miroir
meer-wahr
mirror

Extra words to learn

la brosse à cheveux
bros ah shuh-vuh
hairbrush

la buée
bway
steam

le maquillage
ma-kee-yazh
make-up

les mouchoirs en papier
moosh-wahrs ah(n) pap-yay
tissues

se laver
suh la-vay
washing

la serviette de toilette
sair-vee-et duh twa-let
flannel

la douche
doosh
shower

le papier toilette
pap-yay twa-let
toilet paper

le savon
sa-vo(n)
soap

les toilettes
twa-let
toilet

le robinet
ro-bee-nay
tap

la serviette
de toilette
flannel

le savon
soap

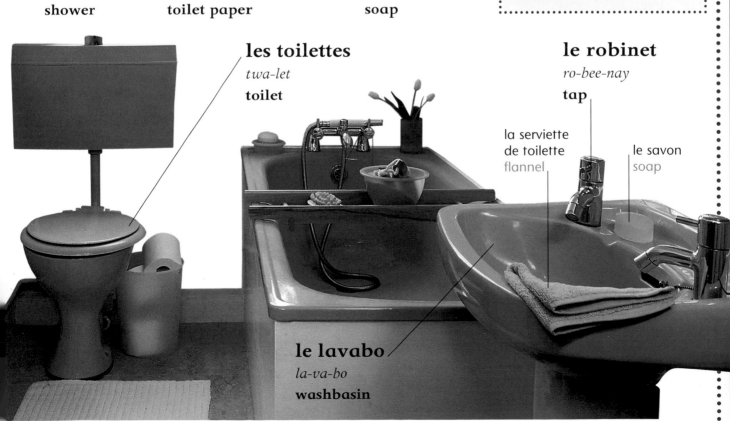

le lavabo
la-va-bo
washbasin

The most expensive bathroom has a gold toilet!

11

Bathroom

le réveil

ray-vaye

alarm clock

le lit

lee

bed

l'oreiller

lo-ray-yay

pillow

la couette

koo-et

duvet

la chaise

shehz

chair

Ma chambre
My bedroom

la commode
kom-mod
chest of drawers

Je dors dans mon lit.

le jeu électronique
zhuh ay-lek-tro-neek
computer game

Nous jouons à un jeu de plateau.

les échecs
chess

la moquette
moh-ket
carpet

Mon chat dort sous mon lit.

Qu'y a-t-il dans l'armoire ?

le tapis
ta-pee
rug

La **moquette** est bleue.

les livres
leev-ruh
books

Je sais jouer de la **guitare**.

l'armoire
larm-wahr
wardrobe

la guitare
ghee-tar
guitar

le cintre
san-truh
coat hanger

la lampe
lahmp
lamp

le miroir
meer-wahr
mirror

13

Le jardin
Garden

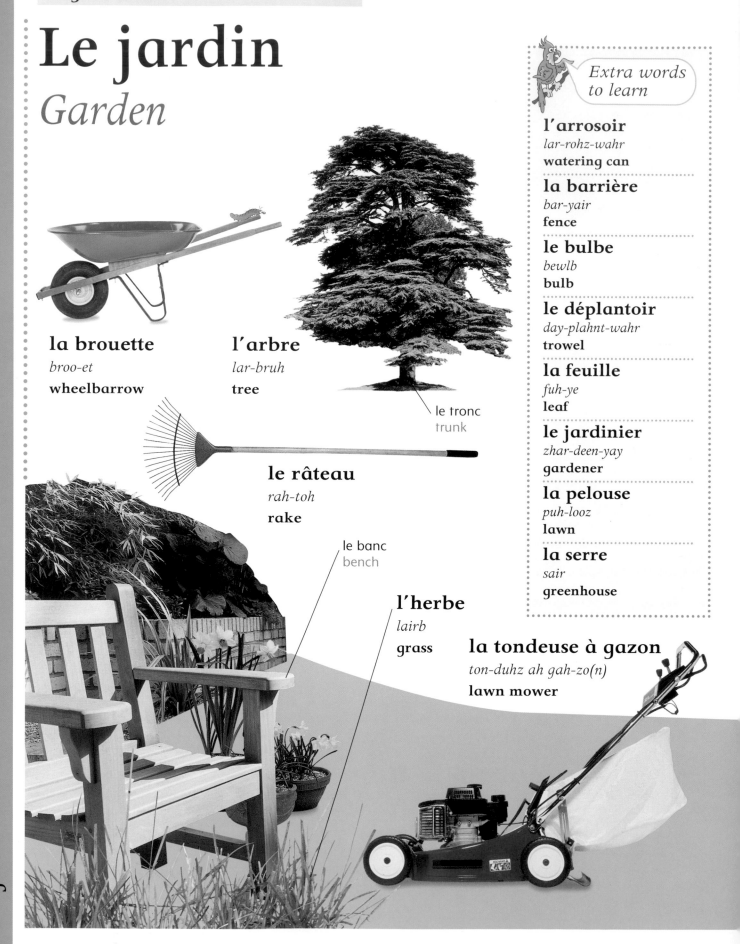

la brouette
broo-et
wheelbarrow

l'arbre
lar-bruh
tree

le tronc
trunk

le râteau
rah-toh
rake

le banc
bench

l'herbe
lairb
grass

la tondeuse à gazon
ton-duhz ah gah-zo(n)
lawn mower

D'habitude, les papillons volent le jour et les papillons de nuit volent la nuit.

Le jardin

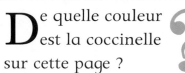

De quelle couleur est la coccinelle sur cette page ?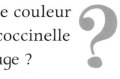

l'escargot
les-kar-goh
snail

le ver
vair
worm

l'aile
wing

le papillon
pa-pee-yo(n)
butterfly

l'abeille
la-baye
bee

la graine
grehn
seed

la coccinelle
kok-see-nel
ladybird

Les **fleurs poussent** dans le **jardin**.

Marie **creuse** dans le **jardin**.

la fleur
fluhr
flower

la chenille
shuh-nee-ye
caterpillar

la terre
tair
soil

la pelle
pel
spade

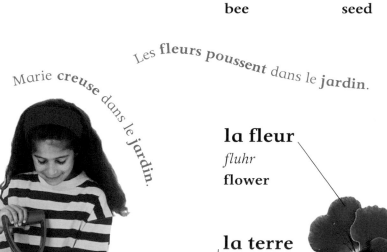

Garden

Usually butterflies fly in the day and moths fly at night.

La vie en ville
City life

l'autobus
lohto-bews
bus

la maison
may-zo(n)
house

> **Q**uelle heure
> **Q**est-il sur
> l'horloge bleue ?
> **?**

le gratte-ciel
grat-syel
skyscraper

*Les **villes** ont de **hauts bâtiments** appelés **gratte-ciel**.*

les appartements
ap-par-tuh-mah(n)
flats

l'horloge
lor-lozh
clock

la rue
rew
street

le magasin
ma-ga-za(n)
shop

◢ Tokyo, au Japon, est la plus grande ville du monde.

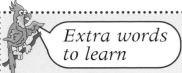

Extra words to learn

l'arrêt de bus
lar-reh duh bews
bus stop

l'autoroute
loh-toh-root
motorway

la banque
bahnk
bank

le café
ka-fay
café

la gare
gar
station

la route
root
road

le trottoir
trot-wahr
pavement

l'usine
lew-zeen
factory

le téléphone
tay-lay-fon
phone

le panneau
pan-noh
sign

les feux de signalisation
fuh duh seen-ya-lee-za-syo(n)
traffic lights

le réverbère
ray-vair-bair
street light

le cinéma
see-nay-ma
cinema

le carrefour
kar-foor
crossing

le taxi
tak-see
taxi

l'hôtel
lo-tel
hotel

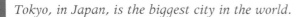

Tokyo, in Japan, is the biggest city in the world.

le cerf-volant
sair-vo-lah(n)
kite

la corde à sauter
kord ah soh-tay
skipping rope

le skate-board
skate-board
skateboard

les fleurs
fluhr
flowers

le tourniquet
toor-nee-kay
roundabout

18

Au parc
In the park

J'adore sauter à la corde !

As-tu un cerf-volant ?

la fille
fee-ye
girl

Trois enfants jouent sur le tourniquet.

Les **oiseaux** chantent.

l'arbre
lar-bruh
tree

la balançoire
ba-lahn-swahr
swing

le garçon
gar-so(n)
boy

le ballon de football
ba-lo(n) duh foot-bohl
football

Mon **jeu préféré** est le football.

le papillon
pa-pee-yo(n)
butterfly

l'oiseau
lwa-zoh
bird

le vélo
vay-lo
bike

la feuille
fuh-ye
leaf

l'herbe
lairb
grass

19

Les loisirs
Hobbies

Mes **fleurs** poussent.

Je suis **prête** à aller *nager*.

faire du camping
fair dew kahm-peeng
camping

la natation
na-ta-syo(n)
swimming

le jardinage
zhar-dee-nazh
gardening

jouer d'un instrument
zhoo-ay dan an-strew-mah(n)
playing an instrument

observer les oiseaux
ob-zair-vay layz wa-zoh
bird-watching

Mathilde s'entraîne tous les jours.

faire de la danse
fair duh la dahnss
dancing

Le surf a commencé à Hawaï, aux Etats-Unis, il y a environ 300 ans.

Les loisirs

Extra words to learn

le chant
shah(n)
singing

collectionner
kol-lek-syo-nay
collecting

le dessin
de-sa(n)
drawing

faire la cuisine
fair la kwee-zeen
cooking

faire du roller
fair dew ro-lair
skating

faire du théâtre
fair dew tay-a-truh
acting

faire du vélo
fair dew vay-lo
cycling

la lecture
lek-tewr
reading

l'écriture
lay-kree-tewr
writing

Quel est ton **Q**loisir préféré ?

le surf
surf
surfing

Je **saute** et je **m'étire** à la gymnastique.

la gymnastique
zheem-nas-teek
gymnastics

prendre une photo
prahn-druh ewn fo-toh
taking a photo

la peinture
pan-tewr
painting

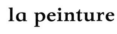

Surfing began in Hawaii, USA, about 300 years ago.

Hobbies

La nourriture

Food

la graine
seed

la peau
skin

la banane

ba-nan

banana

la pastèque

pas-tehk

watermelon

l'orange

lor-ahnzh

orange

la pomme

pom

apple

la tomate

tom-at

tomato

la carotte

ka-rot

carrot

la laitue

lay-tew

lettuce

le chou

shoo

cabbage

Nous **mangeons** des **spaghettis** !

l'assiette
plate

le verre
glass

L'**ananas** est un **fruit**.

le couteau
knife

la fourchette
fork

la chaise
chair

la table
table

l'ananas

lan-an-ass

pineapple

22   La carotte est un légume et une racine !

la pomme de terre
pom duh tair
potato

l'œuf
luhf
egg

le yaourt
ya-oort
yoghurt

le lait
lay
milk

la confiture
kon-fee-tewr
jam

Que manges-tu au petit-déjeuner ?

J'aime le **pain** avec du **miel**.

le pain
pa(n)
bread

le beurre
buhr
butter

le miel
myel
honey

les pâtes
paht
pasta

le riz
rice

la viande
vyanhnd
meat

Extra words to learn

le biscuit
bee-skwee
biscuit

la farine
far-een
flour

le fruit
frwee
fruit

le légume
lay-gewm
vegetable

l'oignon
lohn-yo(n)
onion

le poulet
poo-lay
chicken

la salade
sal-ad
salad

les spaghettis
spa-get-ee
spaghetti

le sucre
soo-kruh
sugar

Food

A carrot is a vegetable and a root!

Les courses
Shopping

le marché
mar-shay
market

le prix
price

l'argent
lar-zhahn
money

le sac
sak
shopping bag

Je **dois acheter** des **œufs.**

Nous **attendons** dans la **queue.**

le panier
pan-yay
basket

le caddie
ka-dee
trolley

Le premier caddie a été inventé il y a plus de 60 ans !

la serveuse
sair-vuhz
waitress

le café
ka-fay
café

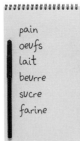

pain
oeufs
lait
beurre
sucre
farine

la liste de courses
leest duh koorss
shopping list

le supermarché
soo-pair-mar-shay
supermarket

la boulangerie
boo-lahn-zhree
bakery

Elle a beaucoup de **sacs** *!*

la librairie
leeb-rair-ee
bookshop

l'acheteuse
lash-tuhz
shopper

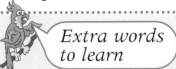
Extra words to learn

l'addition
lad-dee-syo(n)
bill

la caisse
kehss
checkout

en espèces
ah(n) es-pehss
(in) cash

faire les courses
fair lay koorss
to go shopping

le magasin
ma-ga-za(n)
shop

le prix
pree
price

le ticket de caisse
tee-kay duh kehss
receipt

le vendeur
vahn-duhr
shop assistant

Shopping

The first shopping trolley was invented more than 60 years ago!

la boisson
bwa-so(n)
drink

les sandwichs
sahnd-weetsh
sandwiches

**les cartes
d'anniversaire**
kart dan-ee-vair-sair
birthday cards

les bougies
boo-zhee
candles

**le gâteau
d'anniversaire**
gah-toh dan-ee-vair-sair
birthday cake

À la fête
At the party

C'est rigolo de **jouer** avec les **ballons**.

Nous aimons **danser**.

le lecteur de CD
lek-tuhr duh say-day
CD player

le magicien
ma-zhee-sya(n)
magician

Vois-tu le gâteau d'anniversaire ?

les décorations
day-ko-ra-syo(n)
decorations

Bon anniversaire !

C'est incroyable !

Je veux ouvrir les cadeaux.

les cadeaux
ka-doh
presents

Vois-tu les cartes d'anniversaire ?

les ballons
bal-o(n)
balloons

l'appareil photo
lap-pa-ray fo-toh
camera

les biscuits
bee-skwee
biscuits

la glace
glass
ice-cream

les bonbons
bo(n)-bo(n)
sweets

Temps libre
Free time

le jeu de plateau
zhuh duh pla-toh
board game

le ballon
bal-o(n)
ball

le robot
ro-boh
robot

les dés
day
dice

l'ordinateur portable
lor-dee-na-tuhr
por-ta-bluh
laptop

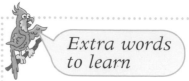

Extra words to learn

cache-cache
kash-kash
hide-and-seek

les cubes
kewb
toy blocks

le jeu
zhuh
game

le jouet
zhoo-way
toy

la marionnette
mar-yon-net
puppet

le masque
mask
mask

partir en vacances
par-teer ah(n) vak-ahns
going on holiday

la poupée
poo-pay
doll

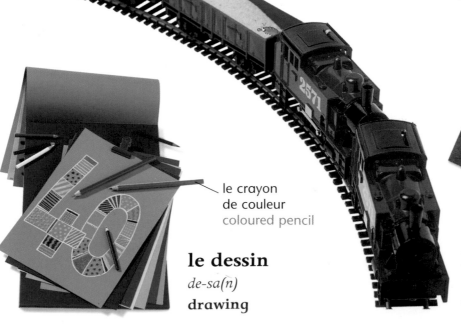

le crayon
de couleur
coloured pencil

le dessin
de-sa(n)
drawing

le puzzle
puh-zluh
puzzle

le train
tra(n)
train

Le premier ordinateur portable a été fabriqué il y a plus de 20 ans.

Temps libre

les cartes
kart
cards

les CD
say-day
CDs

le lecteur de CD
lek-tuhr duh say-day
CD player

le jeu électronique
zhuh ay-lek-tro-neek
computer game

Nous adorons les **spectacles de marionnettes**.

le casque
helmet

Il **bouge** très vite !

faire du roller
fair dew ro-lair
skating (roller)

la marionnette
puppet

**le spectacle
de marionnettes**
*spek-tak-luh
duh mar-yon-net*
puppet show

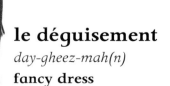

le déguisement
day-gheez-mah(n)
fancy dress

l'ours
en peluche
teddy bear

Aimes-tu
les jeux
électroniques ?

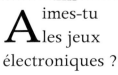

The first laptop was made more than 20 years ago.

Les moyens de transport

Transport

l'avion
lav-yo(n)
plane

le ferry-boat
fay-ree boht
ferry

le bateau à voiles
ba-toh ah vwal
sailing boat

le taxi
tak-see
taxi

Les **gens** voyagent en **autobus**.

le camion
kam-yo(n)
lorry

le vélo
vay-lo
bike

l'autobus
lohto-bews
bus

Pour les secours

To the rescue

l'échelle
ladder

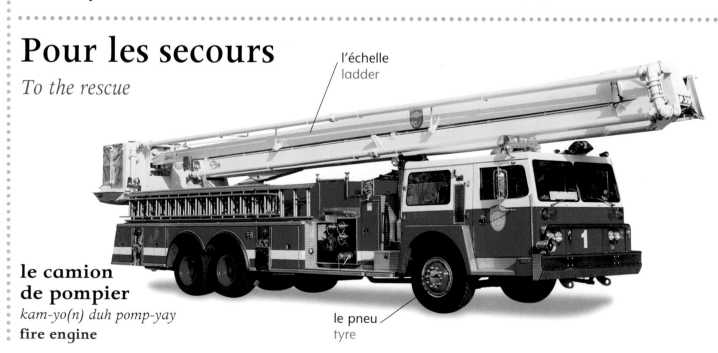

**le camion
de pompier**
kam-yo(n) duh pomp-yay
fire engine

le pneu
tyre

Le camion de pompier le plus rapide a atteint 655 kilomètres-heure en 1998 !

Une **montgolfière** vole dans le ciel.

le panier
basket

la montgolfière

mohn-golf-yair

hot-air balloon

le train

tra(n)

train

*Extra words
to learn*

l'autocar
lohto-kar
coach

le billet
bee-yay
ticket

la camionnette
kam-yon-net
van

le carburant
kar-bew-rah(n)
fuel

la fusée
few-zay
space rocket

le garage
gar-azh
garage

l'horaire
lor-air
timetable

le voyage
vwa-yazh
journey

les bagages
luggage

la voiture

vwah-tewr

car

la moto

moh-toh

motorbike

la roue
wheel

Combien de
roues y a-t-il
sur cette page ?

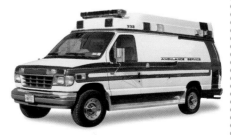

l'hélicoptère
de police

lay-lee-kop-tair duh po-leess

police helicopter

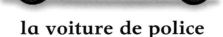

la voiture de police

vwa-tewr duh po-leess

police car

l'ambulance

lahm-bew-lahnss

ambulance

The fastest fire engine reached 655 kilometres per hour (407 mph) in 1998!

Les animaux de la jungle
Jungle animals

l'oiseau-mouche
lwa-zoh-moosh
hummingbird

l'aile
wing

la chauve-souris
shohv soo-ree
bat

le chimpanzé
shahm-pahn-zay
chimpanzee

la fourmi
foor-mee
ant

le papillon
pa-pee-yo(n)
butterfly

l'araignée
lar-ehn-yay
spider

le gorille
go-ree-ye
gorilla

le papillon de nuit
pa-pee-yo(n) duh nwee
moth

Quels animaux **?**
peuvent voler
sur cette page ?

le crocodile
kro-ko-deel
crocodile

32   La jungle la plus grande du monde est en Amérique du Sud.

Le toucan prend la **nourriture** avec son **bec**.

l'œil
eye

le bec
beak

la griffe
claw

la patte
foot

le perroquet
pair-o-kay
parrot

le toucan
too-kah(n)
toucan

Extra words
to learn

l'aigle
lay-gluh
eagle

l'arbre
lar-bruh
tree

la forêt tropicale
for-eh tro-pee-kal
rainforest

l'insecte
lan-sekt
insect

le lézard
lay-zar
lizard

le mammifère
ma-mee-fair
mammal

l'oiseau
lwa-zoh
bird

le scarabée
ska-ra-bay
beetle

le serpent
sair-pah(n)
snake

la grenouille
gruh-noo-ye
frog

les taches
spots

les rayures
stripes

le tigre
tee-gruh
tiger

le léopard
lay-o-par
leopard

Jungle animals

The biggest jungle in the world is in South America.

Les animaux du monde *World animals*

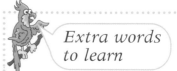

Extra words to learn

le koala
ko-a-la
koala

le daim
da(m)
deer

la patte
paw

le panda
pahn-da
panda

La girafe a un long cou !

le lion
lee-yo(n)
lion

la girafe
zhee-raf
giraffe

l'ours blanc
loorss blah(n)
polar bear

l'alligator
lal-ee-gah-tor
alligator

le babouin
ba-bwa(n)
baboon

la chauve-souris
shohv soo-ree
bat

le faucon
foh-ko(n)
hawk

le loup
loo
wolf

le pélican
pay-lee-kah(n)
pelican

le renard
ruh-nar
fox

la tortue de mer
tor-tew duh mair
turtle

le bec
beak

la queue
tail

le manchot
mahn-shoh
penguin

Combien d'oiseaux y a-t-il sur cette page ?

La girafe a le même nombre d'os que toi dans le cou !

L'éléphant prend la nourriture avec sa trompe.

le chameau
sha-moh
camel

les rayures
stripes

le zèbre
zeh-bruh
zebra

la trompe
trunk

l'éléphant
lay-lay-fah(n)
elephant

le kangourou
kahn-goo-roo
kangaroo

la queue
tail

l'ours
loorss
bear

la griffe
claw

le dauphin
doh-fa(n)
dolphin

la palme
flipper

le rhinocéros
ree-no-say-ros
rhinoceros

A giraffe has the same number of bones in its neck as you!

World animals

35

le champ
shah(m)
field

le tracteur
trak-tuhr
tractor

le blé
blay
wheat

les agneaux
an-yoh
lambs

le chien de berger
shya(n) duh bair-zhay
sheepdog

À la ferme
On the farm

La **fermière** utilise le tracteur.

la fermière
fairm-yair
farmer

Anne donne du **lait** à l'agneau.

La **vache** mange l'herbe dans le champ.

la moissonneuse-batteuse
mwa-son-nuhz bat-tuhz
combine harvester

la barrière
bar-yair
fence

Le cheval est marron et blanc.

Les bébés vaches sont appelés des veaux.

le canard
ka-nar
duck

Le poussin est près de sa mère.

la vache
vash
cow

le foin
fwa(n)
hay

le cheval
shuh-val
horse

le poulet
poo-lay
chicken

les canetons
ka-nuh-to(n)
ducklings

L'océan

Ocean

le bateau de pêche

ba-toh duh pehsh

fishing boat

la mouette

moo-wet

seagull

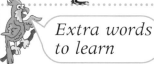 Extra words to learn

l'ancre

lahn-kruh

anchor

la bouée

boo-way

buoy

le canot

kanoh

rowing boat

la mer

mair

sea

la pêche

pehsh

fishing

le port

por

harbour

la vague

vag

wave

la voile
sail

La voile est jaune et violette.

le bateau à voiles

ba-toh ah vwal

sailing boat

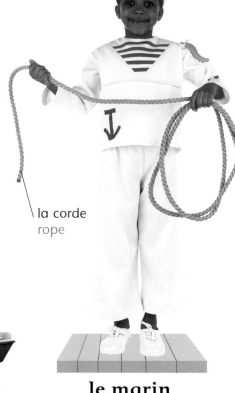

la corde
rope

le marin

mar-a(n)

sailor

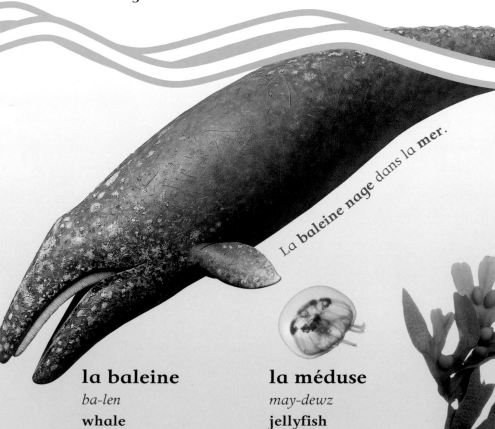

La baleine nage dans la mer.

la baleine

ba-len

whale

la méduse

may-dewz

jellyfish

L'océan

Les océans couvrent presque les trois quarts de la surface de la Terre.

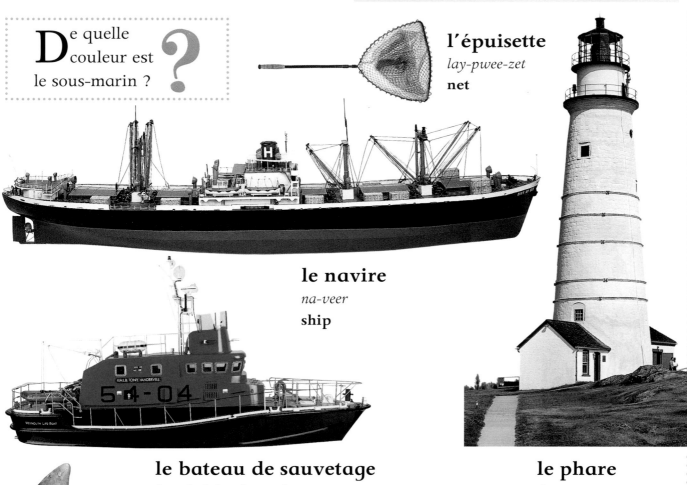

l'épuisette
lay-pwee-zet
net

le navire
na-veer
ship

le bateau de sauvetage
ba-toh duh sohv-tazh
lifeboat

le phare
far
lighthouse

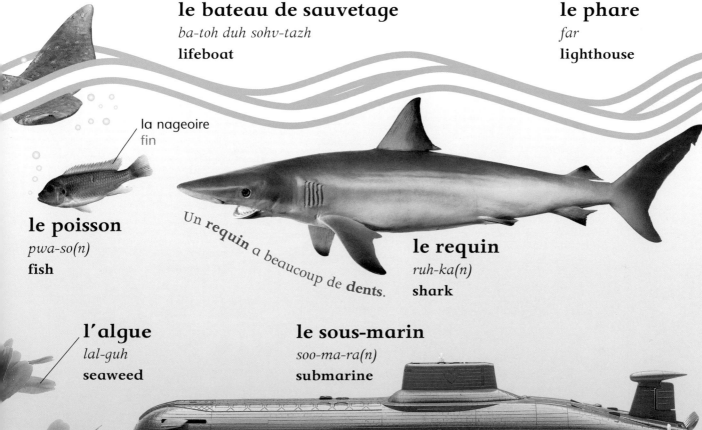

la nageoire
fin

le poisson
pwa-so(n)
fish

Un **requin** a beaucoup de **dents**.

le requin
ruh-ka(n)
shark

l'algue
lal-guh
seaweed

le sous-marin
soo-ma-ra(n)
submarine

Oceans cover nearly three-quarters of the Earth's surface.

Ocean

La nature

Nature

Le **nénuphar pousse** dans l'eau.

le canard
ka-nar
duck

le bec
beak

la plante
plahnt
plant

la libellule
lee-bel-lewl
dragonfly

le nénuphar
nay-new-far
water lily

Beaucoup d'**animaux vivent** près des **étangs**.

le cygne
seen-ye
swan

le crapaud
kra-poo
toad

40   D'habitude, les crapauds ont la peau rugueuse et les grenouilles ont la peau lisse !

Les têtards nagent dans les étangs.

Combien de nénuphars y a-t-il dans l'étang ?

l'antenne
antenna

l'aile
wing

le nid
nee
nest

les têtards
the-tar
tadpoles

la guêpe
gehp
wasp

la mouche
moosh
fly

l'étang
lay-tah(n)
pond

le hibou
ee-boo
owl

la grenouille
gruh-noo-ye
frog

Extra words to learn

l'eau
loh
water

l'habitat
la-bee-ta
habitat

le héron
air-o(n)
heron

l'insecte
lan-sekt
insect

le lapin
lap-a(n)
rabbit

la mauvaise herbe
moh-vayz airb
weed

l'oiseau
lwa-zoh
bird

le papillon
pa-pee-yo(n)
butterfly

Toads usually have rough skin and frogs have smooth skin!

Nature

le seau
soh
bucket

la pelle
pel
spade

le crabe
krab
crab

le coquillage
ko-kee-yazh
shell

les galets
ga-lay
pebbles

À la plage
At the beach

J'adore **nager** dans la **mer** !

Aimes-tu **aller** à la **plage** ?

Je **joue** sous mon **parasol**.

le parasol
umbrella

le rocher
ro-shay
rock

la crème solaire
suncream

les mouettes
moo-wet
seagulls

Nous adorons **jouer** avec le **sable**.

Je porte des **lunettes de natation**.

le maillot de bain
trunks

l'étoile de mer
lay-twal duh mair
starfish

la glace
glass
ice-cream

l'algue
lal-guh
seaweed

Nous **construisons** un **château de sable**.

les lunettes de natation
lew-net duh na-ta-syo(n)
goggles

la chaise longue
shayz long-uh
deck chair

le chapeau
sha-poh
sunhat

le sable
sah-bluh
sand

le château de sable
sha-toh duh sah-bluh
sandcastle

L'école
School

les ciseaux
see-zoh
scissors

les crayons de couleur
kra-yo(n) duh koo-luhr
coloured pencils

le tableau noir
tab-loh nwahr
blackboard

la règle
reh-gluh
ruler

la gomme
gom
rubber

le crayon à papier
kray-o(n) ah pap-yay
pencil

le stylo
stee-loh
pen

le carnet
notebook

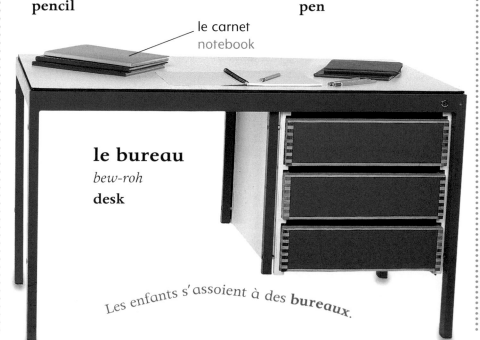

le bureau
bew-roh
desk

*Les enfants s'assoient à des **bureaux**.*

Extra words to learn

l'alphabet
lal-fa-bay
alphabet

la chaise
shehz
chair

le dessin
de-sa(n)
drawing

l'écriture
lay-kree-tewr
writing

la lecture
lek-tewr
reading

le maître
meh-truh
teacher

la salle de classe
sal duh klahss
classroom

les sciences
see-yahnss
science

L'école

44   Le crayon à papier le plus long du monde fait presque 20 mètres de long.

Vois-tu la **pomme** dans le **panier repas** ?

le panier repas
pan-yay ruh-pah
lunch box

C ombien de livres y a-t-il sur cette page ?

les feutres
fuh-truh
felt-tip pens

Trouve ton **pays** sur le **globe**.

le globe
glob
globe

le cahier
ka-yay
exercise book

le cartable
school bag

les livres
leev-ruh
books

l'uniforme scolaire
lew-nee-form sko-lair
school uniform

l'ordinateur
lor-dee-na-tuhr
computer

The longest pencil in the world is almost 20 metres (65 ft) long.

Les sports
Sports

la raquette
rak-et
racket

Je porte un **casque**.

le casque
helmet

la roue
wheel

faire du vélo
fair dew vay-lo
cycling

le ski
skee
skiing

Nous jouons au **basket-ball**.

**le patinage
sur glace**
*pa-tee-nazh
soor glass*
ice skating

la gymnastique
zheem-nas-teek
gymnastics

le tee-shirt
T-shirt

le short
shorts

les baskets
trainers

Delphine **veut marquer** un **but**.

le basket-ball
basket-bohl
basketball

le golf
golf
golf

le football
foot-bohl
football

Il y a environ 28 sports aux Jeux olympiques d'été.

Les sports

l'athlétisme
lat-lay-tee-smah
athletics

le base-ball
bayz-bohl
baseball

l'exercice
lek-sair-seess
exercise

le hockey
ok-ay
hockey

le hockey sur glace
ok-ay soor glass
ice hockey

le judo
zhew-do
judo

le karaté
ka-ra-tay
karate

la natation
na-ta-syo(n)
swimming

Aimes-tu faire du sport ?

la voile
sail

la plongée
plon-zhay
diving

le gilet de sauvetage
life jacket

faire de la voile
fair duh la vwal
sailing

Je **tire** sur les **rames**.

la rame
oar

la balle
ball

le gant
glove

faire de l'aviron
fair duh lav-ee-ro(n)
rowing

la batte
bat
bat

la raquette
racket

le cheval
horse

le rugby
rewg-bee
rugby

la course à pied
koorss ah pyay
running

l'équitation
lay-keet-a-syo(n)
horse riding

le tennis
ten-neess
tennis

There are about 28 sports in the summer Olympic Games.

Sports

Les animaux familiers

Pets

Mon **chien** s'appelle Toby.

la nourriture
food

le chiot

shyoh

puppy

Une **tortue bouge** très **lentement**.

le hamster

am-stair

hamster

la tortue

tor-tew

tortoise

le cochon d'Inde

ko-sho(n) dand

guinea pig

le lapin

lap-(a)n

rabbit

le collier
collar

le chat

sha

cat

le poisson rouge

pwa-so(n) roozh

goldfish

De quelles couleurs sont les poils du cochon d'Inde **?**

Un chat dort environ 16 heures par jour.

les poils
fur

la langue
tongue

le chaton
sha-to(n)
kitten

le chien
shya(n)
dog

la cage
kahzh
cage

le collier
kol-yay
collar

la griffe
greef
claw

la nageoire
nazh-wahr
fin

le panier
pan-yay
basket

la patte
pat
paw

la plume
plewm
feather

le/la vétérinaire
vay-tayr-ee-nair
vet

Un perroquet a des plumes de toutes les couleurs.

le bec
beak

le perroquet
pair-o-kay
parrot

l'oiseau
lwa-zoh
bird

Paul brosse le cheval.

les moustaches
whiskers

la queue
tail

la souris
soo-ree
mouse

le cheval
shuh-val
horse

A cat sleeps about 16 hours a day.

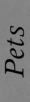

Les couleurs et les formes
Colours and shapes

rouge
roozh
red

orange
or-ahnzh
orange

jaune
zhohn
yellow

vert
vair
green

bleu
bluh
blue

violet
vyo-lay
purple

rose
rohz
pink

marron
mar-o(n)
brown

noir
nwahr
black

courbe
curved

droit
straight

Quelle est ta couleur préférée ?

   Toutes les couleurs sont un mélange de rouge, de jaune et de bleu !

le carré
kar-ray
square

le cercle
sair-kluh
circle

l'arc-en-ciel
rainbow

le triangle
tree-yahn-gluh
triangle

le losange
lo-zahnzh
diamond

l'étoile
lay-twal
star

le rectangle
rek-tahn-gluh
rectangle

Extra words to learn

blanc
blah(n)
white

le cœur
kuhr
heart

coloré
ko-lo-ray
colourful

courbe
koorb
curved

le demi-cercle
duh-mee sair-kluh
semicircle

droit
drwa
straight

l'ovale
lo-val
oval

rond
ro(n)
round

le cube
kewb
cube

le ballon
bal-o(n)
ball

Colours and shapes

All colours are a mixture of red, yellow or blue!

51

Les contraires
Opposites

Ouvre grand !

ouvert
oo-vair
open

rugueux
rew-ghuh
rough

lisse
leess
smooth

mouillé
moo-yay
wet

fermé
fair-may
closed

dry
sec
sek

sale
sal
dirty

propre
prop-ruh
clean

Extra words to learn

léger
lay-zhay
light (weight)

lent
lah(n)
slow

lourd
loor
heavy

nouveau
noo-voh
new

plein
pla(n)
full

rapide
rap-eed
fast

vide
veed
empty

vieux
vyuh
old

Les contraires

La plupart des citrouilles sont orange mais certaines sont blanches ou bleues !

Préfères-tu les boissons chaudes ou froides ?

Une **citrouille** devient **grosse** en **automne**.

froid
frwa
cold

chaud
shoh
hot

gros
groh
fat

Ce **légume** est très **fin**.

fin
fa(n)
thin

doux
doo
soft

dur
dewr
hard

Le **tournesol** a une **grande** tige.

Cette fleur a une **tige courte**.

court
koor
short

grand
grah(n)
tall

petit
puh-tee
small

grand
grah(n)
big

Most pumpkins are orange, but you can grow white and blue ones!

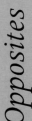

le bonhomme de neige
bon-om duh nehzh
snowman

la neige
nehzh
snow

le bonnet
bon-nay
woolly hat

Il y a beaucoup de vent.

le parapluie
pa-ra-plwee
umbrella

Le temps qu'il fait
Weather

l'automne
loh-ton
autumn

l'hiver
lee-vair
winter

les flocons de neige
flo-ko(n) duh nehzh
snowflakes

J'ai fait un bonhomme de neige.

Je porte un bonnet, une écharpe et des gants.

le printemps
pran-tah(m)
spring

J'ai un **parapluie** jaune.

l'été
lay-tay
summer

le soleil
so-laye
sun

Il fait **chaud** au **soleil**.

la pluie
plwee
rain

le nuage
new-azh
cloud

l'arc-en-ciel
lark-ah(n)-syel
rainbow

les lunettes de soleil
lew-net duh so-laye
sunglasses

la casquette
kas-ket
cap

English A–Z

In this section English words are in alphabetical order, followed by the French translation. There is information after each English word to show you what type of word it is. This will help you to make sentences. In French, nouns (naming words) are either masculine or feminine. If the French word has *un* before it, it is masculine (m), if it has *une*, it is feminine (f).

(n) = noun (a naming word). Either masculine or feminine. Feminine nouns usually have an "e" at the end.

(adj) = adjective (a describing word). These words can change depending whether the noun they are describing is masculine (m) or feminine (f).

(adv) = adverb (a word that gives more information about a verb, an adjective, or another adverb)

(conj) = conjunction (a joining word, e.g., and)

(prep) = preposition (e.g., about)

(pron) = pronoun (e.g., he, she, it)

(article) = (e.g., a, an, the)

A

apple
la pomme

a (article)
un/une
a(n)/ewn

about (adv)
environ
ahn-veer-o(n)

about (prep)
sur
soor

above (prep)
au-dessus de
oh duhs-ew duh

accident (n)
un accident
ak-see-dah(n)

across (prep)
de l'autre côté de
duh loh-truh koh-tay duh

activity (n)
une activité
ak-tee-vee-tay

address (n)
une adresse
a-dress

adult (n)
un/une adulte
ad-ewlt

adventure (n)
une aventure
av-ahn-tewr

aeroplane (n)
un avion
av-yo(n)

after (prep)
après
ap-reh

afternoon (n)
un après-midi
ap-reh mee-dee

again (adv)
encore
ahn-kor

age (n)
l'âge (m)
lahzh

air (n)
l'air (m)
lair

airport (n)
un aéroport
a-ay-ro-por

alarm clock (n)
un réveil
ray-vaye

all (adj)
tout (m) toute (f)
too/toot

alligator (n)
un alligator
al-ee-gah-tor

almost (adv)
presque
presk

alone (adj)
seul (m) seule (f)
suhl

alphabet (n)
l'alphabet (m)
lal-fa-bay

already (adv)
déjà
day-zha

also (adv)
aussi
oh-see

always (adv)
toujours
too-zhoor

amazing (adj)
incroyable
an-krwa-ya-bluh

ambulance (n)
une ambulance
ahm-bew-lahnss

un (article)
un/une
a(n)/ewn

anchor (n)
une ancre
ahn-kruh

and (conj)
et
eh

angry (adj)
en colère
ah(n) ko-lehr

animal (n)
un animal
an-ee-mal

aeroplane
l'avion

ankle (n)
une **cheville**
shuh-vee-ye

answer (n)
une **réponse**
ray-ponss

ant (n)
une **fourmi**
foor-mee

antenna (n)
une **antenne**
ahn-ten

anybody (pron)
n'importe qui
nam-port kee

anything (pron)
n'importe quoi
nam-port kwa

apart (adv)
séparément
say-pa-ray-mah(n)

apartment (n)
un **appartement**
ap-par-tuh-mah(n)

appearance (n)
une **apparence**
ap-par-ahnss

apple (n)
une **pomme**
pom

armchair
le fauteuil

apron (n)
un **tablier**
tab-lee-yay

arch (n)
une **arche**
arsh

area (n)
une **région**
ray-zhyo(n)

arm (n)
un **bras**
bra

armchair (n)
un **fauteuil**
foh-tuh-ye

army (n)
une **armée**
ar-may

around (prep)
autour
oh-toor

arrival (n)
une **arrivée**
ar-ree-vay

arrow (n)
une **flèche**
flehsh

art (n)
l'**art (m)**
lar

astronaut
l'astronaute

artist (n)
un/une **artiste**
ar-teest

assistant (n)
un **assistant**
a-seess-tah(n)

une **assistante**
a-seess-tahnt

astronaut (n)
un/une **astronaute**
astro-noht

astronomer (n)
un/une **astronome**
astro-nom

athletics (n)
l'**athlétisme (m)**
lat-lay-tee-smah

atlas (n)
un **atlas**
at-lahs

attic (n)
un **grenier**
gruhn-yay

aunt (n)
une **tante**
tahnt

autumn (n)
l'**automne (m)**
loh-ton

avocado (n)
un **avocat**
av-o-ka

away (adj)
absent **(m)**
ap-sah(n)

absente **(f)**
ap-sahnt

avocado
l'avocat

B

balloon
le ballon

baboon (n)
un babouin
ba-bwa(n)

baby (n)
un bébé
bay-bay

back (body) (n)
un dos
do

back (adv)
à l'arrière
ah lar-yehr

backpack (n)
un sac à dos
sak ah do

backwards (adv)
en arrière
ah(n) ar-yehr

bad (adj)
mauvais (m)
moh-vay

mauvaise (f)
moh-vayz

badge (n)
un insigne
an-seen-ye

badminton (n)
le badminton
bad-meen-ton

bag (n)
un sac
sak

bakery (n)
une boulangerie
boo-lahn-zhree

balcony (n)
un balcon
bal-ko(n)

ball (n)
un ballon
bal-o(n)

une balle
bal

ballet dancer (n)
un danseur
classique
dahn-suhr kla-seek

une danseuse
classique
dahn-suhz kla-seek

balloon (n)
un ballon
bal-o(n)

banana (n)
une banane
ba-nan

bear
l'ours

band (n)
une bande
bahnd

bank (money) (n)
une banque
bahnk

bank (river) (n)
une rive
reev

barbecue (n)
un barbecue
bar-buhk-yew

barn (n)
une grange
grahnzh

baseball (n)
le base-ball
bayz-bohl

basket (n)
un panier
pan-yay

basketball (n)
le basket-ball
basket-bohl

bat (animal) (n)
une chauve-souris
shohv soo-ree

bat (sports) (n)
une batte
bat

bath (n)
une baignoire
bayn-wahr

bathroom (n)
une salle de bains
sal duh ba(n)

battery (n)
une pile
peel

battle (n)
une bataille
bat-ah-ye

beach (n)
une plage
plazh

bat
la chauve-souris

bead (n)
une perle
pairl

beak (n)
un bec
behk

beans (n)
les haricots blancs
ar-ee-koh blah(n)

bear (n)
un ours
oorss

beard (n)
une barbe
barb

beautiful (adj)
beau (m) belle (f)
boh/bell

beauty (n)
la beauté
boh-tay

because (conj)
parce que
par-suh-kuh

bed (n)
un lit
lee

bedroom (n)
une chambre
shahm-bruh

bee (n)
une abeille
a-baye

beetle (n)
un scarabée
ska-ra-bay

B

A
C
D
E
F
G
H
I
J
K
L
M
N
O
P
Q
R
S
T
U
V
W
X
Y
Z

before (prep)
avant
av-ah(n)

behind (prep)
derrière
dair-yehr

bell (n)
une cloche
klosh

below (prep)
au-dessous de
oh-duh-soo duh

belt (n)
une ceinture
san-tewr

bench (n)
un banc
bah(n)

best (adj)
mieux
myuh

better (adj)
meilleur (m)
meilleure (f)
may-yuhr

between (prep)
entre
ahn-truh

big (wide) (adj)
gros (m) grosse (f)
groh/grohss

bike
le vélo

saddle
la selle

pedal
la pédale

tyre
le pneu

wheel
la roue

binoculars
les jumelles

big (tall) (adj)
grand (m)
grah(n)
grande (f)
grahnd

bike (n)
un vélo
vay-lo

bill (n)
une addition
ad-dee-syo(n)

billion
milliard
meel-yar

bin (n)
une poubelle
poo-bell

binoculars (n)
les jumelles
zhew-mel

bird (n)
un oiseau
wa-zoh

birthday (n)
un anniversaire
an-ee-vair-sair

birthday cake (n)
un gâteau
d'anniversaire
gah-toh dan-ee-vair-sair

birthday card (n)
une carte
d'anniversaire
kart dan-ee-vair-sair

biscuit (n)
un biscuit
bee-skwee

black (adj)
noir (m) noire (f)
nwahr

blackboard (n)
un tableau noir
tab-loh nwahr

blanket (n)
une couverture
koo-vair-tewr

blonde (adj)
blond (m)
bloh(n)
blonde (f)
blohnd

blood (n)
le sang
sah(n)

blouse (n)
un chemisier
shuh-meez-yay

blue (adj)
bleu (m) bleue (f)
bluh

board (notice) (n)
un panneau
pan-noh

board game (n)
un jeu de plateau
zhuh duh pla-toh

boat (n)
un bateau
ba-toh

B

A C D E F G H I J K L M N O P Q R S T U V W X Y Z

body (n)
un corps
kor

bone (n)
un os
oss

book (n)
un livre
leev-ruh

bookshop (n)
une librairie
leeb-rair-ee

boot (n)
une botte
bot

boring (adj)
ennuyeux (m)
ahn-wee-yuh

ennuyeuse (f)
ahn-wee-yuhz

bottle (n)
une bouteille
boo-taye

bottom (n)
le fond
foh(n)

bowl (cereal) (n)
un bol
bol

box (n)
une boîte
bwat

boy (n)
un garçon
gar-so(n)

boyfriend (n)
un petit ami
puh-tee-ta-mee

bracelet (n)
un bracelet
bra-slay

brain (n)
un cerveau
sair-voh

branch (n)
une branche
brahnsh

brave (adj)
courageux (m)
koor-a-zhuh

courageuse (f)
koor-a-zhuhz

bread (n)
un pain
pa(n)

break (n)
une pause
pohz

breakfast (n)
un petit-déjeuner
puh-tee day-zhuh-nay

breeze (n)
une brise
breez

bridge (n)
un pont
po(n)

bubbles
les bulles

butterfly
le papillon

bright (adj)
brillant (m)
bree-yah(n)

brillante (f)
bree-yahnt

broken (adj)
cassé (m) cassée (f)
kah-say

broom (n)
un balai
ba-lay

brother (n)
un frère
frair

brown (adj)
marron
mar-o(n)

bubble (n)
une bulle
bewl

bucket (n)
un seau
soh

buggy (pushchair) (n)
une poussette
poo-set

building (n)
un bâtiment
bah-tee-mah(n)

bulb (light) (n)
une ampoule
ahm-pool

bulb (plant) (n)
un bulbe
bewlb

buoy (n)
une bouée
boo-way

bus (n)
un autobus
ohto-bews

bus stop (n)
un arrêt de bus
ar-reh duh bews

bush (n)
un buisson
bwee-so(n)

business (n)
les affaires
a-fair

busy (adj)
occupé (m)
occupée (f)
ok-ew-pay

but (conj)
mais
may

butter (n)
le beurre
buhr

butterfly (n)
un papillon
pa-pee-yo(n)

button (n)
un bouton
boo-to(n)

C

cake
le gâteau

cabbage (n)
un **chou**
shoo

café (n)
un **café**
ka-fay

cage (n)
une **cage**
kahzh

cake (n)
un **gâteau**
gah-toh

calculator (n)
une **calculatrice**
kal-kew-la-treess

calendar (n)
un **calendrier**
kal-ahn-dree-yay

calf (n)
un **veau**
voh

calm (adj)
calme
kalm

camel (n)
un **chameau**
sha-moh

camera (n)
un **appareil photo**
ap-pa-ray fo-toh

can (n)
un **bidon**
bee-do(n)

candle (n)
une **bougie**
boo-zhee

canoe (n)
un **canoë**
kan-o-ay

cap (n)
une **casquette**
kas-ket

capital (n)
une **capitale**
ka-pee-tal

car (n)
une **voiture**
vwah-tewr

card (n)
une **carte**
kart

cardboard (n)
le **carton**
kar-to(n)

cards (n)
les **cartes**
kart

careful (adj)
prudent (m)
prew-dah(n)
prudente (f)
prew-dahnt

carpet (n)
une **moquette**
moh-ket

carrot (n)
une **carotte**
ka-rot

cart (n)
une **charrette**
sha-ret

cash (n)
en **espèces**
ah(n) es-pehss

cassette (n)
une **cassette**
ka-set

cat (n)
un **chat**
sha

caterpillar (n)
une **chenille**
shuh-nee-ye

cave (n)
une **grotte**
grot

CD (n)
un **CD**
say-day

CD player (n)
un **lecteur de CD**
lek-tuhr duh say-day

ceiling (n)
un **plafond**
pla-fo(n)

cellar (n)
une **cave**
kav

centre (n)
le **centre**
sahn-truh

cereal (n)
une **céréale**
sair-ay-al

certain (adj)
certain (m)
sair-ta(n)
certaine (f)
sair-tehn

chain (n)
une **chaîne**
shehn

chair (n)
une **chaise**
shehz

challenge (n)
un **défi**
day-fee

change (n)
un **changement**
shahnzh-mah(n)

cheap (adj)
bon marché
bo(n) mar-shay

checkout (n)
une **caisse**
kehss

cheese (n)
un **fromage**
fro-mazh

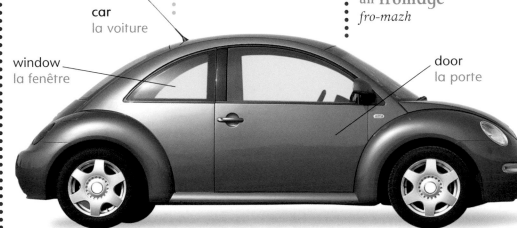

car
la voiture

window
la fenêtre

door
la porte

A B C D E F G H I J K L M N O P Q R S T U V W X Y Z

A
B
C
D
E
F
G
H
I
J
K
L
M
N
O
P
Q
R
S
T
U
V
W
X
Y
Z

cheetah (n)
un **guépard**
gay-par

chef (n)
un/une **chef**
shef

chemist (shop) (n)
une **pharmacie**
far-ma-see

chess (n)
les **échecs**
ay-shek

chest (n)
une **poitrine**
pwa-treen

**chest of
drawers (n)**
une **commode**
kom-mod

chewing gum (n)
un **chewing-gum**
shweeng gom

chick (n)
un **poussin**
poo-sa(n)

chicken (n)
un **poulet**
poo-lay

child (n)
un/une **enfant**
ahn-fah(n)

children (n)
les **enfants**
ahn-fah(n)

chimney (n)
une **cheminée**
shuh-mee-nay

chimpanzee (n)
un **chimpanzé**
shahm-pahn-zay

chin (n)
un **menton**
mahn-to(n)

chips (n)
les **frites**
freet

chocolate (n)
le **chocolat**
sho-ko-la

Christmas (n)
Noël
no-el

church (n)
une **église**
ayg-leess

cinema (n)
un **cinéma**
see-nay-ma

circle (n)
un **cercle**
sair-kluh

circus (n)
un **cirque**
seerk

city (n)
une **ville**
veel

classroom (n)
une **salle de classe**
sal duh klahss

claw (n)
une **griffe**
greef

clean (adj)
propre
prop-ruh

clear (adj)
clair (m) claire (f)
klair

clever (adj)
intelligent (m)
an-tel-lee-zhah(n)

intelligente (f)
an-tel-lee-zhahnt

cliff (n)
une **falaise**
fu-lehz

cloak (n)
une **cape**
kap

clock (n)
une **horloge**
or-lozh

close (near) (adj)
proche
prosh

closed (adj)
fermé (m) fermée (f)
fair-may

cloth (n)
un **tissu**
tee-soo

clothes (n)
les **vêtements**
veht-mah(n)

cloud (n)
un **nuage**
new-azh

cloudy (adj)
nuageux (m)
new-azh-uh

nuageuse (f)
new-azh-uhz

clown (n)
un **clown**
kloon

coach (n)
un **autocar**
ohto-kar

coast (n)
une **côte**
koht

coat (n)
un **manteau**
mahn-toh

coat hanger (n)
un **cintre**
san-truh

coffee (n)
le **café**
ka-fay

coin (n)
une **pièce**
pyehs

cold (adj)
froid (m)
frwa

froide (f)
frwad

collar (n)
un **collier**
kol-yay

colour (n)
une **couleur**
koo-luhr

coloured pencil (n)
un **crayon de
couleur**
kra-yo(n) duh koo-luhr

computer
l'ordinateur

hard drive
le disque dur

keyboard
le clavier

screen
l'écran

mouse mat
le tapis de souris

mouse
la souris

compass
la boussole

computer game (n)
un **jeu électronique**
zhuh ay-lek-tro-neek

concert (n)
un **concert**
kon-sair

continent (n)
un **continent**
kon-tee-nah(n)

controls (n)
les **commandes**
ko-mahnd

cooker (n)
une **cuisinière**
kwee-zeen-yair

cool (adj)
frais (m)
fray
fraîche (f)
frehsh

corner (n)
un **coin**
kwa(n)

correct (adj)
juste
zhewst

costume (n)
un **costume**
kos-tewm

cotton (n)
le **coton**
ko-to(n)

cough (n)
une **toux**
too

country (n)
un **pays**
pay-ee

countryside (n)
la **campagne**
kahm-pan-ye

colourful (adj)
coloré (m)
colorée (f)
ko-lo-ray

comb (n)
un peigne
pain-ye

combine harvester (n)
une moissonneuse-batteuse
mwa-son-nuhz bat-tuhz

comfortable (adj)
confortable
kon-for-ta-bluh

comic (n)
un comique
ko-meek

compass (n)
une boussole
boo-sol

computer (n)
un ordinateur
or-dee-na-tuhr

crab
le crabe

cousin (n)
un **cousin**
koo-za(n)
une **cousine**
koo-zeen

cow (n)
une **vache**
vash

cowboy (n)
un **cow-boy**
koh-boye

crab (n)
un **crabe**
krab

crane (n)
une **grue**
grew

crayon (n)
un **crayon de couleur**
kray-o(n) duh koo-luhr

cream (n)
la **crème**
krehm

creature (n)
une **bête**
beht

crew (n)
un **équipage**
ay-kee-pazh

crocodile (n)
un **crocodile**
kro-ko-deel

crop (n)
une **récolte**
ray-kolt

crossing (n)
un **carrefour**
kar-foor

crowded (adj)
bondé (m)
bondée (f)
bon-day

crown (n)
une **couronne**
koo-ron

cube (n)
un **cube**
kewb

cup (n)
une **tasse**
tahss

cupboard (n)
un **placard**
pla-kar

curious (adj)
curieux (m)
kew-ree-uh
curieuse (f)
kew-ree-uhz

curly (adj)
frisé (m) frisée (f)
free-zay

curtain (n)
un **rideau**
ree-doh

curved (adj)
courbe
koorb

cushion (n)
un **coussin**
koo-sa(n)

customer (n)
un **client**
klee-ah(n)
une **cliente**
klee-ahnt

crown
la couronne

A B C D E F G H I J K L M N O P Q R S T U V W X Y Z

A B C **D** E F G H I J K L M N O P Q R S T U V W X Y Z

D

daisy
la pâquerette

dad (n)
papa
pa-pa

dairy (adj)
laitier (m) laitière (f)
layt-yay/layt-yair

daisy (n)
une pâquerette
pak-uh-ret

dancer (n)
un danseur
dahn-suhr

une danseuse
dahn-suhz

dandelion (n)
un pissenlit
pee-sahn-lee

danger (n)
un danger
dahn-zhay

dangerous (adj)
dangereux (m)
dahn-zhay-ruh

dangereuse (f)
dahn-zhay-ruhz

dark (adj)
sombre
som-bruh

date (n)
une date
dat

daughter (n)
une fille
fee-ye

day (n)
un jour
zhoor

dead (adj)
mort (m) morte (f)
mor/mort

deaf (adj)
sourd (m) sourde (f)
soor/soord

dear (special, expensive) (adj)
cher (m) chère (f)
shair

deck (boat) (n)
un pont
po(n)

deck chair (n)
une chaise longue
shayz long-uh

decoration (n)
une décoration
day-ko-ra-syo(n)

deep (adj)
profond (m)
pro-fo(n)

profonde (f)
pro-fond

deer (n)
un daim
da(m)

delicious (adj)
délicieux (m)
day-lee-syuh

délicieuse (f)
day-lee-syuhz

dentist (n)
un/une dentiste
dahn-teest

date (n)
un désert
day-zair

desk (n)
un bureau
bew-roh

dessert (n)
un dessert
duh-sair

diagram (n)
un diagramme
dya-gram

diamond (shape) (n)
un losange
lo-zahnzh

diary (n)
un journal
zhoor-nal

dice (n)
les dés
day

dictionary (n)
un dictionnaire
deek-syo-nair

different (adj)
différent (m)
dee-fay-rah(n)

différente (f)
dee-fay-rahnt

difficult (adj)
difficile
dee-fee-seel

digital (adj)
digital (m)
digitale (f)
dee-zhee-tal

dining room (n)
une salle à manger
sal ah mahn-zhay

dinner (n)
un dîner
dee-nay

dinosaur (n)
un dinosaure
dee-noh-zor

direction (n)
une direction
dee-rek-syo(n)

directly (adv)
directement
dee-rek-tuh-mah(n)

dirty (adj)
sale
sal

disabled (adj)
handicapé (m)
handicapée (f)
ahn-dee-ka-pay

disco (n)
une discothèque
dee-sko-tek

distance (n)
une distance
dee-stahnss

diving (n)
la plongée
plon-zhay

divorced (adj)
divorcé (m)
divorcée (f)
dee-vor-say

doctor (n)
un médecin
may-duh-sa(n)

dog (n)
un chien
shya(n)

doll (n)
une poupée
poo-pay

dolphin (n)
un dauphin
doh-fa(n)

dome (n)
un dôme
dohm

door (n)
une porte
port

downstairs (adv)
au rez-de-chaussée
oh ray-du-shoh-say

dragon (n)
un dragon
dra-go(n)

dragonfly (n)
une libellule
lee-bel-lewl

drawer (n)
un tiroir
teer-wahr

drawing (act of) (n)
le dessin
de-sa(n)

drawing pin (n)
une punaise
pew-nehz

dream (n)
un rêve
rehv

dress (n)
une robe
rob

drink (n)
une boisson
bwa-so(n)

drinking straw (n)
une paille
pah-ye

drop (n)
une goutte
goot

drum (n)
un tambour
tahm-boor

drum kit (n)
une batterie
bat-tree

dry (adj)
sec (m) sèche (f)
sek/sehsh

duck (n)
un canard
ka-nar

duckling (n)
un caneton
ka-nuh-to(n)

during (prep)
pendant
pahn-dah(n)

dust (n)
la poussière
poo-syair

duvet (n)
une couette
koo-et

DVD (n)
un DVD
day-vay-day

DVD player (n)
un lecteur de DVD
lek-tuhr duh day-vay-day

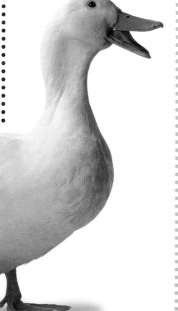

duck
le canard

E

egg
l'œuf

each (adj)
chaque
shak

eagle (n)
un aigle
ay-gluh

ear (n)
une oreille
o-raye

earache (n)
une otite
o-teet

early (adv)
tôt
toh

earring (n)
une boucle
d'oreille
book-luh do-raye

Earth (planet) (n)
la Terre
tair

earthworm (n)
un ver de terre
vair duh tair

east (n)
l'est (m)
lest

easy (adj)
facile
fa-seel

echo (n)
un écho
ay-ko

edge (n)
le bord
bor

effect (n)
un effet
ay-fay

egg (n)
un œuf
uhf

elbow (n)
un coude
kood

electrical (adj)
électrique
ay-lek-treek

elephant (n)
un éléphant
ay-lay-fah(n)

email (n)
un e-mail
ee-mail

email address (n)
une adresse
électronique
a-dress ay-lek-tro-neek

emergency (n)
une urgence
ewr-zhahnss

empty (adj)
vide
veed

encyclopedia (n)
une encyclopédie
ahn-see-klo-pay-dee

end (final part) (n)
la fin
fa(n)

A B C **D** **E** F G H I J K L M N O P Q R S T U V W X Y Z

A B C D **E** F G H I J K L M N O P Q R S T U V W X Y Z

English (n)
l'anglais (m)
lahn-glay

enough (adj)
assez
a-say

enthusiastic (adj)
enthousiaste
ahn-too-zee-ast

entrance (n)
une entrée
ahn-tray

envelope (n)
une enveloppe
ahn-vlop

environment (n)
un environnement
ahn-vee-ron-mah(n)

equal (adj)
égal (m) égale (f)
ay-gal

equator (n)
l'équateur (m)
lay-kwa-tuhr

equipment (n)
le matériel
ma-tay-ree-el

even (adv)
même
mehm

evening (n)
un soir
swahr

event (n)
un événement
ay-vayn-mah(n)

exercise
l'exercice

arm
le bras

hand
la main

stamp
le timbre

Tour Eiffel
Champ-de-Mars
75007 Paris
FRANCE

envelope
l'enveloppe

address
l'adresse

every (adj)
tous
too

everybody (pron)
tout le monde
too luh mond

everyday (adv)
tous les jours
too lay zhoor

everything (pron)
tout
too

everywhere (adv)
partout
par-too

exam (n)
un examen
eg-za-ma(n)

excellent (adj)
excellent (m)
ek-say-lah(n)
excellente (f)
ek-say-lahnt

exchange (n)
un échange
ay-shahnzh

excited (adj)
excité (m)
excitée (f)
ek-see-tay

exercise (n)
un exercice
ek-sair-seess

exercise book (n)
un cahier
ka-yay

expedition (n)
une expédition
ek-spay-dee-syo(n)

expensive (adj)
cher (m) chère (f)
shair

experiment (n)
une expérience
ek-spay-ree-ahnss

expert (n)
un expert
ek-spair
une experte
ek-spairt

explorer (n)
un explorateur
ek-splor-a-tuhr
une exploratrice
ek-splor-a-treess

explosion (n)
une explosion
ek-sploh-zyo(n)

extinct (adj)
éteint (m)
ay-ta(n)
éteinte (f)
ay-tant

extra (adj)
supplémentaire
soo-play-mahn-tair

extremely (adv)
extrêmement
ek-streh-muh-mah(n)

eye (n)
un œil
uh-ye

eyebrow (n)
un sourcil
soor-seel

eyelash (n)
un cil
seel

leg
la jambe

foot
le pied

F

fancy dress
le déguisement

fabulous (adj)
fabuleux (m)
fa-bew-luh

fabuleuse (f)
fa-bew-luhz

face (n)
un visage
vee-zazh

fact (n)
un fait
fay

factory (n)
une usine
ew-zeen

faint (pale) (adj)
faible
fay-bluh

fair (n)
une foire
fwahr

false (adj)
faux (m) fausse (f)
foh/fohss

family (n)
une famille
fa-mee-ye

famous (adj)
célèbre
say-lay-bruh

fancy dress (n)
un déguisement
day-gheez-mah(n)

fantastic (adj)
fantastique
fan-tas-teek

far (adv)
loin
lwa(n)

farm (n)
une ferme
fairm

farmer (n)
un fermier
fairm-yay

une fermière
fairm-yair

fashion (n)
la mode
mod

fashionable (adj)
à la mode
ah la mod

fast (adv)
rapide
rap-eed

fat (adj)
gros (m) grosse (f)
groh/grohss

father (n)
un père
pair

favourite (adj)
préféré (m)
préférée (f)
pray-fair-ay

feather (n)
une plume
plewm

felt-tip pen (n)
un feutre
fuh-truh

female (human) (n)
une femme
fam

fence (n)
une barrière
bar-yair

ferry (n)
un ferry-boat
fay-ree boht

festival (n)
une fête
feht

field (n)
un champ
shah(m)

film (n)
un film
feelm

film star (n)
une vedette
de cinéma
vuh-det duh see-nay-ma

fin (n)
une nageoire
nazh-wahr

fine (adv)
bien
bya(n)

finger (n)
un doigt
dwa

fire (n)
un feu
fuh

fire engine (n)
un camion
de pompier
kam-yo(n) duh pomp-yay

firefighter (n)
un pompier
pomp-yay

first (adv)
d'abord
da-bor

first (adj)
premier (m)
pruhm-yay

première (f)
pruhm-yair

first aid (n)
les premiers
secours
pruhm-yay suh-koor

fish (n)
un poisson
pwa-so(n)

fishing (n)
la pêche
pehsh

fishing boat (n)
un bateau de pêche
ba-toh duh pehsh

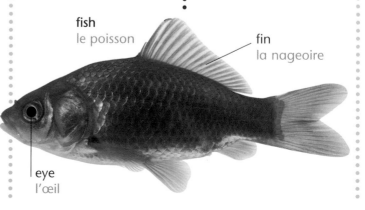

fish
le poisson

fin
la nageoire

eye
l'œil

A B C D E **F** G H I J K L M N O P Q R S T U V W X Y Z

67

football
le ballon de football

fit (adj)
en forme
ah(n) form

flag (n)
un **drapeau**
dra-poh

flannel (n)
une **serviette**
de toilette
sair-vee-et duh twa-let

flat (building) (n)
un **appartement**
ap-par-tuh-mah(n)

flat (adj)
plat (m) plate (f)
pla/plat

fleece (n)
une **polaire**
po-lair

flipper (n)
une **palme**
palm

flock (of sheep) (n)
un **troupeau**
troo-poh

flood (n)
une **inondation**
in-on-da-syo(n)

floor (n)
le **sol**
sol

flour (n)
la **farine**
far-een

flower (n)
une **fleur**
fluhr

flute (n)
une **flûte**
flewt

fly (n)
une **mouche**
moosh

fog (n)
le **brouillard**
broo-yar

food (n)
la **nourriture**
noo-ree-tewr

foot (human) (n)
un **pied**
pyay

foot (animal) (n)
une **patte**
pat

football (ball) (n)
un **ballon**
de football
ba-lo(n) duh foot-bohl

football (game) (n)
le **football**
foot-bohl

foreign (adj)
étranger (m)
ay-trahn-zhay
étrangère (f)
ay-trahn-zhair

forest (n)
une **forêt**
fo-reh

fork (n)
une **fourchette**
foor-shet

forward (adv)
en **avant**
ah(n) av-ah(n)

fox (n)
un **renard**
ruh-nar

frame (n)
un **cadre**
kah-druh

free time (n)
le **temps libre**
tah(n) lee-bruh

freedom (n)
la **liberté**
lee-bair-tay

freezer (n)
un **congélateur**
kon-zhay-la-tuhr

French (n)
le **français**
frahn-say

fresh (adj)
frais (m) fraîche (f)
fray/frehsh

fridge (n)
un **réfrigérateur**
ray-free-zhair-a-tuhr

friend (n)
un **ami**, une **amie**
a-mee

friendly (adj)
amical (m)
amicale (f)
a-mee-kal

frightened (adj)
effrayé (m)
effrayée (f)
eh-fray-yay

frog (n)
une **grenouille**
gruh-noo-ye

from (prep)
de
duh

front door (n)
une **porte d'entrée**
port dahn-tray

fruit (n)
un **fruit**
frwee

frying pan (n)
une **poêle**
pwal

fuel (n)
le **carburant**
kar-bew-rah(n)

full (adj)
plein (m) pleine (f)
pla(n)/plen

fun (n)
un **amusement**
am-ewz-mah(n)

fun (adj)
rigolo
ree-go-loh

fur (n)
les **poils**
pwal

furniture (n)
les **meubles**
muh-bluh

future (n)
l'**avenir** (m)
lav-neer

frog
la grenouille

A B C D E **F** G H I J K L M N O P Q R S T U V W X Y Z

G

globe
le globe

game (n)
un jeu
zhuh

garage (n)
un garage
gar-azh

garden (n)
un jardin
zhar-da(n)

gardener (n)
un jardinier
zhar-deen-yay

une jardinière
zhar-deen-yair

gardening (n)
le jardinage
zhar-dee-nazh

gas (n)
le gaz
gahz

gentle (adj)
doux (m) douce (f)
doo/dooss

gently (adv)
doucement
dooss-mah(n)

giant (n)
un géant
zhay-ah(n)

giraffe (n)
une girafe
zhee-raf

girl (n)
une fille
fee-ye

girlfriend (n)
une petite amie
puh-teet a-mee

glacier (n)
un glacier
glass-yay

glass (drink) (n)
un verre
vair

glasses (n)
les lunettes
lew-net

globe (n)
un globe
glob

glove (n)
un gant
gah(n)

glue (n)
la colle
kol

goal (n)
un but
bewt

goat (n)
une chèvre
shay-vruh

God (n)
Dieu
dyuh

goggles (n)
les lunettes
de natation
lew-net duh
na-ta-syo(n)

gold (n)
l'or (m)
lor

goldfish (n)
un poisson rouge
pwa-so(n) roozh

golf (n)
le golf
golf

good (adj)
bon (m) bonne (f)
bo(n)/bon

gorilla (n)
un gorille
go-ree-ye

government (n)
un gouvernement
goo-vairn-mah(n)

grandfather (n)
un grand-père
grah(n)-pair

grandmother (n)
une grand-mère
grah(n)-mair

grandparents (n)
les grands-parents
grah(n)-par-ah(n)

grape (n)
le raisin
ray-za(n)

grass (n)
l'herbe (f)
lairb

grasshopper (n)
une sauterelle
soht-rel

great (adj)
formidable
for-mee-da-bluh

green (adj)
vert (m) verte (f)
vair/vairt

greenhouse (n)
une serre
sair

ground (n)
la terre
tair

group (n)
un groupe
groop

guide (n)
un guide
gheed

guinea pig (n)
un cochon d'Inde
ko-sho(n) dand

guitar (n)
une guitare
ghee-tar

gymnastics (n)
la gymnastique
zheem-nas-teek

guitar
la guitare

A
B
C
D
E
F
G
H
I
J
K
L
M
N
O
P
Q
R
S
T
U
V
W
X
Y
Z

69

H

handbag
le sac à main

habitat (n)
un habitat
a-bee-ta

hair (n)
les cheveux
shuh-vuh

hairbrush (n)
une brosse
à cheveux
bros ah shuh-vuh

hairdresser's (n)
un coiffeur
kwa-fuhr

une coiffeuse
kwa-fuhz

hairy (adj)
poilu (m) poilue (f)
pwa-lew

half (n)
une moitié
mwat-yay

hall (n)
un couloir
kool-wahr

hamster (n)
un hamster
am-stair

hand (n)
une main
ma(n)

handbag (n)
un sac à main
sak ah ma(n)

handkerchief (n)
un mouchoir
moosh-wahr

hang-glider (n)
un deltaplane
delta-plan

happy (adj)
content (m)
kon-tah(n)

contente (f)
kon-tahnt

harbour (n)
un port
por

hat
le chapeau

hard (adj)
dur (m) dure (f)
dewr

hard drive (n)
un disque dur
deesk dewr

hare (n)
un lièvre
lyeh-vruh

harvest (n)
une moisson
mwa-so(n)

hat (n)
un chapeau
sha-poh

hawk (n)
un faucon
foh-ko(n)

hay (n)
le foin
fwa(n)

he (pron)
il
eel

head (n)
une tête
teht

headache (n)
un mal de tête
mal duh teht

healthy (adj)
en bonne santé
ah(n) bon sahn-tay

heart (n)
un cœur
kuhr

heat (n)
la chaleur
sha-luhr

heavy (adj)
lourd (m) lourde (f)
loor/loord

helicopter (n)
un hélicoptère
ay-lee-kop-tair

hamster
le hamster

helmet (n)
un casque
kask

help (n)
une aide
ehd

her/his (adj)
son (m) sa (f)
so(n)/sa

her/him (pron)
la (her) le (him)
l' (before a vowel)
la/luh/l

hero (n)
un héros
air-o

heron (n)
un héron
air-o(n)

hers/his (pron)
le sien (m)
luh sya(n)

la sienne (f)
la syen

hi
salut
sa-lew

hide-and-seek (n)
cache-cache
kash-kash

high (adj)
haut (m) haute (f)
oh/oht

hill (n)
une colline
kol-leen

hip (n)
une hanche
ahnsh

historical (adj)
historique
ee-stor-eek

history (n)
l'histoire (f)
leest-wahr

hive (n)
une ruche
rewsh

hobby (n)
un loisir
lwa-zeer

hockey (n)
le hockey
ok-ay

hole (n)
un trou
troo

holiday (n)
les vacances
vak-ahnss

home (n)
la maison
may-zo(n)

homework (n)
les devoirs
duhv-wahr

honey (n)
le miel
myel

hood (n)
une capuche
kap-ewsh

horn (n)
une corne
korn

horrible (adj)
horrible
o-ree-bluh

horse (n)
un cheval
shuh-val

horse riding (n)
l'équitation (f)
lay-keet-a-syo(n)

hospital (n)
un hôpital
o-pee-tal

hot (adj)
chaud (m)
shoh

chaude (f)
shohd

hot-air balloon (n)
une montgolfière
mohn-golf-yair

hot chocolate (n)
un chocolat chaud
sho-ko-la shoh

hot dog (n)
un hot-dog
ot-dog

hotel (n)
un hôtel
o-tel

hour (n)
l'heure (f)
luhr

house (n)
une maison
may-zo(n)

how (adv)
comment
ko-mah(n)

huge (adj)
énorme
ay-norm

human (n)
un être humain
eh-truh ew-ma(n)

hummingbird (n)
un oiseau-mouche
wa-zoh-moosh

honey
le miel

hungry (adj)
affamé (m)
affamée (f)
af-fa-may

hurricane (n)
un ouragan
oo-ra-gah(n)

husband (n)
un mari
ma-ree

hut (n)
une cabane
ka-ban

horse
le cheval

A B C D E F G **H** I J K L M N O P Q R S T U V W X Y Z

island
l'île

I (pron)
je/j'
zhuh/zh

ice (n)
la glace
glass

ice-cream (n)
une glace
glass

ice cube (n)
un glaçon
glass-o(n)

ice-cream
la glace

ice hockey (n)
le hockey sur glace
ok-ay soor glass

ice lolly (n)
un esquimau
es-kee-moh

ice skating (n)
le patinage
sur glace
pa-tee-nazh soor glass

idea (n)
une idée
ee-day

ill (adj)
malade
ma-lad

illness (n)
une maladie
ma-la-dee

immediately (adv)
tout de suite
too-duh-sweet

important (adj)
important (m)
am-por-tah(n)

importante (f)
am-por-tahnt

impossible (adj)
impossible
am-po-see-bluh

information (n)
une information
an-for-ma-syo(n)

ingredient (n)
un ingrédient
an-gray-diah(n)

injury (n)
une blessure
bless-ewr

ink (n)
l'encre (f)
lahn-kruh

insect (n)
un insecte
an-sekt

inside (prep)
à l'intérieur de
ah lan-tayr-yuhr duh

instruction (n)
une instruction
an-strewk-syo(n)

instrument (n)
un instrument
an-strew-mah(n)

interesting (adj)
intéressant (m)
an-tair-ay-sah(n)

intéressante (f)
an-tair-ay-sahnt

international (adj)
international (m)
internationale (f)
an-tair-na-syo-nal

Internet (n)
l'Internet (m)
lin-tair-net

into (prep)
dans
dah(n)

invitation (n)
une invitation
an-vee-ta-syo(n)

iron (clothes) (n)
un fer à repasser
fair ah ruh-pah-say

island (n)
une île
eel

its (adj)
son (m) sa (f)
so(n)/sa

it's (it is)
c'est
say

ice skating
le patinage sur glace

dress
la robe

leg
la jambe

J

jug
la cruche

jacket (n)
un **blouson**
bloo-zo(n)

jam (n)
la **confiture**
kon-fee-tewr

jeans (n)
un **jean**
jeen

jellyfish (n)
une **méduse**
may-dewz

jet (n)
un **avion à réaction**
av-yo(n) ah ray-ak-syo(n)

jewel (n)
un **bijou**
bee-zhoo

jewellery (n)
les **bijoux**
bee-zhoo

job (n)
un **emploi**
am-plwa

joke (n)
une **blague**
blag

journey (n)
un **voyage**
vwa-yazh

judo (n)
le **judo**
zhew-doh

jug (n)
une **cruche**
krewsh

juice (n)
le **jus**
zhew

jumper (n)
un **pull-over**
pewl-o-vair

jungle (n)
la **jungle**
zhahn-gluh

just (adv)
juste
zhewst

jeans
le jean

K

kite
le cerf-volant

kangaroo (n)
un **kangourou**
kahn-goo-roo

karate (n)
le **karaté**
ka-ra-tay

kettle (n)
une **bouilloire**
booy-wahr

key (n)
une **clé**
klay

keyboard (n)
un **clavier**
klav-yay

kind (gentle) (adj)
gentil (m)
zhahn-tee
gentille (f)
zhahn-teeye

kind (type) (n)
une **sorte**
sort

king (n)
un **roi**
rwa

kiss (n)
un **baiser**
bay-zay

kitchen (n)
une **cuisine**
kwee-zeen

kite (n)
un **cerf-volant**
sair-vo-lah(n)

kitten (n)
un **chaton**
sha-to(n)

knee (n)
un **genou**
zhuh-noo

knife (n)
un **couteau**
koo-toh

knight (n)
un **chevalier**
shuh-val-yay

knot (n)
un **nœud**
nuh

koala (n)
un **koala**
ko-a-la

tail
la queue

kitten
le chaton

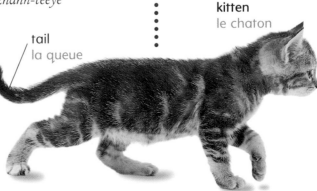

L

lemon
le citron

ladder (n)
une **échelle**
ay-shell

ladybird (n)
une **coccinelle**
kok-see-nel

lake (n)
un **lac**
lak

lamb (n)
un **agneau**
an-yoh

lamp (n)
une **lampe**
lahmp

land (n)
un **terrain**
tair-ra(n)

language (n)
une **langue**
lahn-guh

laptop (n)
un **ordinateur portable**
or-dee-na-tuhr por-ta-bluh

last (adj)
dernier (m)
dairn-yay
dernière (f)
dairn-yair

late (adv)
en retard
ah(n) ruh-tar

law (n)
une **loi**
lwa

lawn (n)
une **pelouse**
puh-looz

lawn mower (n)
une **tondeuse à gazon**
ton-duhz ah gah-zo(n)

lazy (adj)
paresseux (m)
pa-re-suh
paresseuse (f)
pa-re-suhz

leaf (n)
une **feuille**
fuh-ye

leather (adj)
en cuir
ah(n) kweer

left (adj)
gauche
gohsh

left-handed (adj)
gaucher (m)
goh-shay
gauchère (f)
goh-shair

leg (n)
une **jambe**
zhahmb

lemon (n)
un **citron**
see-tro(n)

lemonade (n)
une **limonade**
lee-mon-ad

leopard (n)
un **léopard**
lay-o-par

lesson (n)
une **leçon**
le-so(n)

letter (n)
une **lettre**
let-truh

letter box (n)
une **boîte aux lettres**
bwat oh let-truh

lettuce (n)
une **laitue**
lay-tew

level (adj)
plat (m) plate (f)
pla/plat

library (n)
une **bibliothèque**
bee-blee-yo-tek

lid (n)
un **couvercle**
koo-vair-kluh

life (n)
la **vie**
vee

lifeboat (n)
un **bateau de sauvetage**
ba-toh duh sohv-tazh

lifeguard (n)
un **surveillant de baignade**
soor-vay-ah(n) duh bayn-yad

life jacket (n)
un **gilet de sauvetage**
zhee-lay duh sohv-tazh

lift (n)
un **ascenseur**
a-sahn-suhr

light (not heavy) (adj)
léger (m) légère (f)
lay-zhay/lay-zhehr

light (pale) (adj)
clair (m) claire (f)
klair

light (n)
une **lumière**
lewm-yair

lighthouse (n)
un **phare**
far

lightning (n)
un **éclair**
ay-klair

like (prep)
comme
kom

line (n)
une **ligne**
leen-ye

lion (n)
un **lion**
lee-yo(n)

liquid (n)
un **liquide**
lee-keed

list (n)
une **liste**
leest

little (adj)
petit (m) petite (f)
puh-tee/puh-teet

lizard
le lézard

living room (n)
un **salon**
sal-o(n)

lizard (n)
un **lézard**
lay-zar

long (adj)
long (m) longue (f)
lo(n)/lon-guh

loose (adj)
ample
ahm-pluh

lorry (n)
un **camion**
kam-yo(n)

(a) lot (adj)
beaucoup
boh-koo

loud (adj)
bruyant (m)
brew-yah(n)

bruyante (f)
brew-yahnt

lovely (adj)
adorable
a-do-ra-bluh

low (adj)
bas (m) basse (f)
bah/bahss

lucky (adj)
chanceux (m)
shahn-suh

chanceuse (f)
shahn-suhz

luggage (n)
les **bagages**
bag-azh

lunch (n)
le **déjeuner**
day-zhuh-nay

lunch box (n)
un **panier repas**
pan-yay ruh-pah

M

mask
le masque

machine (n)
une **machine**
ma-sheen

magazine (n)
un **magazine**
ma-ga-zeen

magician (n)
un **magicien**
ma-zhee-sya(n)

une **magicienne**
ma-zhee-syen

magnet (n)
un **aimant**
eh-mah(n)

magnetic (adj)
magnétique
man-yet-eek

magnifying glass (n)
une **loupe**
loop

mail (n)
la **poste**
post

tail
la queue

main (adj)
principal (m)
principale (f)
prahn-see-pal

make-up (n)
le **maquillage**
ma-kee-yazh

male (human) (n)
un **homme**
om

mammal (n)
un **mammifère**
ma-mee-fair

man (n)
un **homme**
om

map (n)
une **carte**
kart

marbles (toy) (n)
les **billes**
bee-ye

mark (n)
une **note**
noht

market (n)
un **marché**
mar-shay

married (adj)
marié (m) mariée (f)
mar-yay

mask (n)
un **masque**
mask

mat (n)
un **petit tapis**
puh-tee ta-pee

match (football) (n)
un **match**
match

matchbox (n)
une **boîte d'allumettes**
bwat dal-lew-met

maths (n)
les **mathématiques**
ma-tay-ma-teek

maybe (adv)
peut-être
puht-eh-truh

me (pron)
me/m' (vowel)
muh/m

meal (n)
un **repas**
ruh-pah

meaning (n)
un **sens**
sahnss

measurement (n)
une **mesure**
muh-zewr

meat (n)
la **viande**
vyahnd

medicine (n)
un **médicament**
may-dee-ka-mah(n)

melon (n)
un **melon**
muh-lo(n)

menu (n)
la **carte**
kart

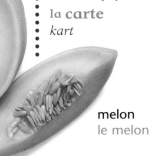

melon
le melon

A B C D E F G H I J K L **M** N O P Q R S T U V W X Y Z

milk shake
le milk-shake

mess (n)
le désordre
day-zor-druh

message (n)
un message
mess-azh

microwave (n)
un micro-ondes
mee-kro-ond

middle (n)
le milieu
meel-yuh

midnight (n)
minuit
mee-nwee

milk (n)
le lait
lay

milk shake (n)
un milk-shake
meelk-shayk

million
million
meel-yo(n)

mineral (n)
un minéral
mee-nay-ral

minute (n)
une minute
mee-newt

mirror (n)
un miroir
meer-wahr

mistake (n)
une erreur
er-ruhr

mitten (n)
une mitaine
mee-tehn

mixture (n)
un mélange
may-lahnzh

mobile phone (n)
un téléphone portable/
un portable
tay-lay-fon por-ta-bluh

modelling clay (n)
la pâte à modeler
paht ah mod-lay

money (n)
l'argent (m)
lar-zhah(n)

monkey (n)
un singe
sanzh

monster (n)
un monstre
mon-struh

month (n)
un mois
mwa

mitten
la mitaine

moon (n)
la lune
lewn

more than
plus que
plews kuh

morning (n)
le matin
ma-ta(n)

mosque (n)
une mosquée
mos-kay

moth (n)
un papillon de nuit
pa-pee-yo(n) duh nwee

mother (n)
une mère
mair

motor (n)
un moteur
mo-tuhr

motorbike (n)
une moto
moh-toh

motorway (n)
une autoroute
oh-toh-root

mountain (n)
une montagne
mon-tan-ye

mountain bike (n)
un V. T. T.
vay-tay-tay

mouse (animal) (n)
une souris
soo-ree

mouse (computer) (n)
une souris
soo-ree

mouse mat (n)
un tapis de souris
ta-pee duh soo-ree

moustache (n)
une moustache
moo-stash

mouth (n)
une bouche
boosh

mud (n)
la boue
boo

muddy (adj)
boueux (m)
boo-uh

boueuse (f)
boo-uhz

mug (n)
une tasse
tahss

mum (n)
maman
mah-mah(n)

museum (n)
un musée
mew-zay

mushroom (n)
un champignon
shahm-peen-yo(n)

music (n)
la musique
mew-zeek

musician (n)
un musicien
mew-zee-sya(n)

une musicienne
mew-zee-syen

my (adj)
mon (m) ma (f)
mo(n)/ma

mushroom
le champignon

N

necklace
le collier

nail (n)
un **ongle**
ong-luh

name (n)
un **nom**
no(m)

narrow (adj)
étroit (m) étroite (f)
ay-trwa/ay-trwat

nature (n)
la **nature**
nat-ewr

naughty (adj)
vilain (m)
vee-la(n)

vilaine (f)
veelehn

nest
le nid

near (prep)
près de
preh duh

nearly (adv)
presque
presk

neck (n)
un **cou**
koo

necklace (n)
un **collier**
kol-yay

needle (n)
une **aiguille**
ehg-wee-ye

neighbour (n)
un **voisin**
vwa-za(n)

une **voisine**
vwa-zeen

nephew (n)
un **neveu**
nuh-vuh

nest (n)
un **nid**
nee

net (n)
une **épuisette**
ay-pwee-zet

never (adv)
jamais
zha-may

new (adj)
nouveau (m)
noo-voh

nouvelle (f)
noo-vel

news (n)
les **nouvelles**
noo-vel

newspaper (n)
un **journal**
zhoor-nal

next (adj)
prochain (m)
prosh-a(n)

prochaine (f)
prosh-ehn

nice (adj)
sympathique
sam-pa-teek

niece (n)
une **nièce**
nyehs

night (n)
la **nuit**
nwee

nobody (pron)
personne
pair-son

noisy (adj)
bruyant (m)
brew-yah(n)

bruyante (f)
brew-yahnt

noodles (n)
les **nouilles**
noo-ye

north (n)
le **nord**
nor

nose (n)
un **nez**
nay

note (n)
un **billet**
bee-yay

noodles
les nouilles

notebook (n)
un **carnet**
kar-nay

nothing (n/pron)
rien
rya(n)

now (adv)
maintenant
mehn-tuh-nah(n)

nowhere (adv)
nulle part
newl par

number (n)
un **nombre**
nom-bruh

nurse (n)
une **infirmière**
an-feerm-yair

nursery (n)
une **crèche**
krehsh

felt-tip pen
le feutre

notebook
le carnet

A B C D E F G H I J K L M **N** O P Q R S T U V W X Y Z

O

ocean
l'océan

oar (n)
une **rame**
ram

object (n)
un **objet**
ob-zhay

ocean (n)
un **océan**
o-say-ah(n)

office (n)
un **bureau**
bew-roh

often (adv)
souvent
soo-vah(n)

oil (n)
l'**huile** (f)
lweel

old (adj)
vieux (m) **vieille** (f)
vyuh/vyay

old person (n)
une **personne âgée**
pair-son ah-zhay

Olympic Games (n)
les **Jeux olympiques**
zhuz o-leem-peek

on top of (prep)
sur
soor

onion (n)
un **oignon**
ohn-yo(n)

only (adv)
seulement
suhl-mah(n)

open (adj)
ouvert (m)
oo-vair
ouverte (f)
oo-vairt

opening hours (n)
les **heures
d'ouverture**
uhr doo-vair-tewr

onion
l'oignon

orange juice
le jus d'orange

operation (n)
une **opération**
o-pair-a-syo(n)

opposite (n)
un **contraire**
kon-trair

opposite (prep)
en face de
ah(n) fass duh

or (conj)
ou
oo

**orange (colour)
(adj)**
orange
or-ahnzh

orange (fruit) (n)
une **orange**
or-ahnzh

orange juice (n)
un **jus d'orange**
zhew dor-ahnzh

orchestra (n)
un **orchestre**
or-ke-struh

other (adj)
autre
oh-truh

ouch!
aïe !
eye-ye

orange
l'orange

our (adj)
notre (m/f)
no-truh

out of (prep)
hors de
or duh

outside (adv)
dehors
duh-or

oval (n)
un **ovale**
o-val

oven (n)
un **four**
foor

oven glove (n)
un **gant de cuisine**
gah(n) duh kwee-zeen

over there (adv)
là-bas
la-bah

owl (n)
un **hibou**
ee-boo

own (adj)
propre
pro-pruh

owl
le hibou

P

paint tin
le pot de peinture

page (n)
une **page**
pazh

paint (n)
la **peinture**
pan-tewr

paint brush (n)
un **pinceau**
pan-soh

paint tin (n)
un **pot de peinture**
poh duh pan-tewr

pair (n)
une **paire**
pair

palm tree (n)
un **palmier**
palm-yay

pancake (n)
une **crêpe**
krehp

panda (n)
un **panda**
pahn-da

paper (n)
le **papier**
pap-yay

paper clip (n)
un **trombone**
trom-bon

paper towel (n)
un **essuie-tout**
es-swee too

parade (n)
un **défilé**
day-fee-lay

parent (n)
un **parent**
par-ah(n)

park (n)
un **parc**
park

parrot (n)
un **perroquet**
pair-o-kay

part (n)
une **partie**
par-tee

partner (n)
un/une **camarade**
ka-ma-rad

party (n)
une **fête**
feht

passenger (n)
un **passager**
pah-sa-zhay

une **passagère**
pah-sa-zhair

passport (n)
un **passeport**
pah-spor

past (history) (n)
le **passé**
pah-say

past (prep)
après
ap-reh

pasta (n)
les **pâtes**
paht

path (n)
un **chemin**
shuh-ma(n)

patient (adj)
patient (m)
pa-sya(n)

patiente (f)
pa-syant

patient (n)
un **patient**
pa-sya(n)

une **patiente**
pa-syant

pattern (n)
un **motif**
mo-teef

pavement (n)
un **trottoir**
trot-wahr

paw (n)
une **patte**
pat

pay (n)
un **salaire**
sa-lair

pea (n)
un **petit pois**
puh-tee pwa

peace (n)
la **paix**
pay

pelican
le pélican

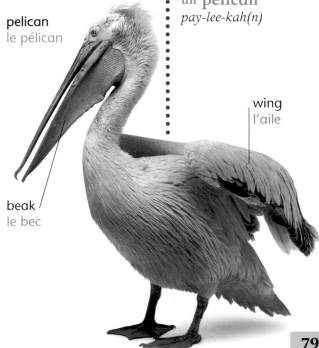

beak
le bec

wing
l'aile

pear
la poire

peaceful (adj)
tranquille
trahn-keel

peanut (n)
une **cacahuète**
ka-ka-weht

pear (n)
une **poire**
pwahr

pebble (n)
un **galet**
ga-lay

pedal (n)
une **pédale**
pay-dal

pelican (n)
un **pélican**
pay-lee-kah(n)

A B C D E F G H I J K L M N O **P** Q R S T U V W X Y Z

pen (n)
un **stylo**
stee-loh

pencil (n)
un **crayon à papier**
kray-o(n) ah pap-yay

pencil case (n)
une **trousse**
trooss

penguin (n)
un **manchot**
mahn-shoh

people (n)
les **gens** (pl)
zhah(n)

pepper (n)
le **poivre**
pwa-vruh

perfect (adj)
parfait (m)
par-fay

parfaite (f)
par-feht

perhaps (adv)
peut-être
puh-teh-truh

person (n)
une **personne**
pair-son

pet (n)
un **animal familier**
an-ee-mal fa-meel-yay

petrol (n)
l'**essence** (f)
le-sahns

phone (n)
un **téléphone**
tay-lay-fon

photo (n)
une **photo**
fo-toh

piano (n)
un **piano**
piano

picnic (n)
un **pique-nique**
peek-neek

picture (n)
une **image**
ee-mazh

pinecone
la pomme de pin

piano
le piano

piece (n)
un **morceau**
mor-soh

pig (n)
un **cochon**
ko-sho(n)

pillow (n)
un **oreiller**
o-ray-yay

pilot (n)
un **pilote**
pee-lot

pineapple (n)
un **ananas**
an-an-ass

pinecone (n)
une **pomme de pin**
pom duh pa(n)

pine tree (n)
un **pin**
pa(n)

pink (adj)
rose
rohz

pizza (n)
une **pizza**
peed-za

place (n)
un **endroit**
ahn-drwa

plane (n)
un **avion**
av-yo(n)

planet (n)
une **planète**
plan-eht

plant (n)
une **plante**
plahnt

plastic (adj)
en **plastique**
ah(n) plas-teek

plastic bag (n)
un **sac en plastique**
sak ah(n) plas-teek

plate (n)
une **assiette**
a-syet

platform (n)
un **quai**
kay

play (n)
une **pièce**
de théâtre
pyehs duh tay-a-truh

player (n)
un **joueur**
zhoo-uhr

une **joueuse**
zhoo-uhz

pine tree
le pin

playground (n)
une **cour de récréation**
koor duh ray-kray-a-syo(n)

playtime (n)
une **récréation**
ray-kray-a-syo(n)

please (adv)
s'il te plaît
seel tuh pleh

plug (for bath) (n)
une **bonde**
bond

plug (electric) (n)
une **prise électrique**
preez ay-lek-treek

pocket (n)
une **poche**
posh

pocket money (n)
l'**argent de poche** (m)
lar-zhah(n) duh posh

point (n)
un **point**
pwa(n)

polar bear (n)
un **ours blanc**
oorss blah(n)

pole (post) (n)
un **poteau**
po-toh

police (n)
la **police**
po-leess

police car (n)
une **voiture de police**
vwa-tewr duh po-leess

police helicopter (n)
un **hélicoptère de police**
ay-lee-kop-tair duh po-leess

pond (n)
un **étang**
ay-tah(n)

poor (adj)
pauvre
poh-vruh

popular (adj)
populaire
po-pew-lair

possible (adj)
possible
po-see-bluh

postbox (n)
une **boîte aux lettres**
bwat oh let-truh

postcard (n)
une **carte postale**
kart pos-tal

postcode (n)
un **code postal**
kohd pos-tal

poster (n)
une **affiche**
af-feesh

postman (n)
un **facteur**
fak-tuhr
une **factrice**
fak-treess

post office (n)
un **bureau de poste**
bew-roh duh post

potato (n)
une **pomme de terre**
pom duh tair

powder (n)
la **poudre**
poo-druh

present (n)
un **cadeau**
ka-doh

president (n)
un **président**
pray-zee-dah(n)

puppet
la marionnette

pretty (adj)
joli (m) **jolie** (f)
zho-lee

price (n)
un **prix**
pree

prince (n)
un **prince**
pranss

princess (n)
une **princesse**
pran-sess

prize (n)
un **prix**
pree

probably (adv)
probablement
pro-bab-luh-mah(n)

problem (n)
un **problème**
prob-lehm

programme (TV) (n)
une **émission**
ay-mee-syo(n)

project (n)
un **projet**
pro-zhay

pudding (n)
un **dessert**
duh-sair

pumpkin (n)
une **citrouille**
see-troo-ye

pupil (n)
un/une **élève**
ay-lehv

puppet (n)
une **marionnette**
mar-yon-net

puppet show (n)
un **spectacle de marionnettes**
spek-tak-luh duh mar-yon-net

puppy (n)
un **chiot**
shyoh

purple (adj)
violet (m) **violette** (f)
vyo-lay/vyo-let

purse (n)
un **porte-monnaie**
port-mo-nay

puzzle (n)
un **puzzle**
puh-zluh

pyjamas (n)
un **pyjama**
pee-zha-ma

purse
le porte-monnaie

A B C D E F G H I J K L M N O **P** Q R S T U V W X Y Z

81

Q R

A B C D E F G H I J K L M N O P **Q R** S T U V W X Y Z

quarter (n)
un **quart**
kar

queen (n)
une **reine**
rehn

question (n)
une **question**
kest-yo(n)

queue (n)
une **queue**
kuh

quickly (adv)
vite
veet

quiet (adj)
silencieux (m)
see-lahn-syuh
silencieuse (f)
see-lahn-syuhz

quietly (adv)
tranquillement
trahn-keel-mah(n)

quiz (n)
un **quiz**
kweez

queen
la reine

rabbit (n)
un **lapin**
lap-a(n)

race (n)
une **course**
koorss

racing car (n)
une **voiture**
de course
vwa-tewr duh koorss

racket (n)
une **raquette**
rak-et

radio (n)
une **radio**
rad-yo

railway station (n)
une **gare**
gar

rain (n)
la **pluie**
plwee

rainbow (n)
un **arc-en-ciel**
ark-ah(n)-syel

raincoat (n)
un **imperméable**
am-pair-may-a-bluh

racing car
la voiture
de course

rainforest (n)
la **forêt tropicale**
for-eh tro-pee-kal

rake (n)
un **râteau**
rah-toh

raspberry (n)
une **framboise**
frahm-bwaz

rat (n)
un **rat**
ra

reading (n)
la **lecture**
lek-tewr

ready (adj)
prêt (m)
preh
prête (f)
preht

real (adj)
réel (m) réelle (f)
ray-el

really (adv)
vraiment
vray-mah(n)

receipt (n)
un **ticket de caisse**
tee-kay duh kess

recipe (n)
une **recette**
ruh-set

rectangle (n)
un **rectangle**
rek-tahn-gluh

red (adj)
rouge
roozh

remote control (n)
une **télécommande**
tay-lay-kom-mahnd

**report
(for school) (n)**
un **exposé**
ek-spoh-zay

rescue (n)
les **secours**
suh-koor

restaurant (n)
un **restaurant**
res-tor-ah(n)

rhinoceros (n)
un **rhinocéros**
ree-no-say-ros

ribbon (n)
un **ruban**
rew-bah(n)

rice (n)
le **riz**
ree

rich (adj)
riche
reesh

riding (n)
l'**équitation (f)**
lay-kee-ta-syo(n)

**right (not left)
(adj)**
droit (m) droite (f)
drwa/drwat

**right (correct)
(adj)**
exact (m) exacte (f)
eg-zakt

ring (n)
une **bague**
bag

ripe (adj)
mûr (m) **mûre** (f)
mewr

river (n)
une **rivière**
reev-yehr

road (n)
une **route**
root

robot (n)
un **robot**
ro-boh

rock (n)
un **rocher**
ro-shay

rocket (n)
une **fusée**
few-zay

roll (n)
un **petit pain**
puh-tee pa(n)

roof (n)
un **toit**
twa

room (n)
une **pièce**
pyehs

root (n)
une **racine**
ra-seen

rope (n)
une **corde**
cord

rose (n)
une **rose**
rohz

rough (adj)
rugueux (m)
rew-ghuh

rugueuse (f)
rew-ghuhz

round (adj)
rond (m)
ro(n)

ronde (f)
rond

roundabout (n)
un **tourniquet**
toor-nee-kay

route (n)
un **trajet**
tra-zhay

rowing boat (n)
un **canot**
kanoh

rubber (eraser) (n)
une **gomme**
gom

rubber band (n)
un **élastique**
ay-la-steek

rubbish (n)
les **ordures**
or-dewr

rucksack (n)
un **sac à dos**
sak ah doh

rug (n)
un **tapis**
ta-pee

rugby (n)
le **rugby**
rewg-bee

ruler (measure) (n)
une **règle**
reh-gluh

running (n)
la **course à pied**
koorss ah pyay

S

saddle
la selle

sack (n)
un **sac**
sak

sad (adj)
triste
treest

saddle (n)
une **selle**
sel

safe (adj)
en **sécurité**
ah(n) say-kew-ree-tay

sail (n)
une **voile**
vwal

sailing boat (n)
un **bateau à voiles**
ba-toh ah vwal

sailor (n)
un **marin**
mar-a(n)

salad (n)
une **salade**
sal-ad

salt (n)
le **sel**
sel

same (adj)
même
mehm

sand (n)
le **sable**
sah-bluh

sandal (n)
une **sandalette**
sahn-da-let

sandcastle (n)
un **château**
de sable
sha-toh duh sah-bluh

sandwich (n)
un **sandwich**
sahnd-weetsh

saucepan (n)
une **casserole**
kass-rol

scarf (n)
une **écharpe**
ay-sharp

school (n)
l' **école** (f)
lay-kol

school bag (n)
un **cartable**
kar-ta-bluh

school uniform (n)
un **uniforme**
scolaire
ew-nee-form sko-lair

science (n)
les **sciences**
see-yahnss

scarf
l'écharpe

A B C D E F G H I J K L M N O P Q **R** **S** T U V W X Y Z

scissors
les ciseaux

scientist (n)
un/une
scientifique
see-yahn-tee-feek

scissors (n)
les ciseaux
see-zoh

score (n)
un score
skor

screen (n)
un écran
ay-krah(n)

sea (n)
la mer
mair

seafood (n)
les fruits de mer
frwee duh mair

seagull (n)
une mouette
moo-wet

seal (n)
un phoque
fok

sea lion (n)
un lion de mer
lee-yo(n) duh mair

seaside (n)
le bord de la mer
bor duh la mair

season (n)
une saison
seh-zo(n)

seaweed (n)
une algue
al-guh

second (2nd) (adj)
deuxième
duhz-yehm

seed (n)
une graine
grehn

semicircle (n)
un demi-cercle
duh-mee sair-kluh

shadow (n)
une ombre
om-bruh

shallow (adj)
peu profond (m)
puh pro-fo(n)

peu profonde (f)
puh pro-fond

shampoo (n)
un shampooing
shahm-pwa(n)

shape (n)
une forme
form

shark (n)
un requin
ruh-ka(n)

sharp (adj)
aigu (m) aiguë (f)
ehg-ew

she (pron)
elle
el

sheep (n)
un mouton
moo-to(n)

sheepdog (n)
un chien de berger
shya(n) duh bair-zhay

sheet (for bed) (n)
un drap
dra

shelf (n)
une étagère
ay-ta-zhehr

shell (n)
un coquillage
ko-kee-yazh

shiny (adj)
brillant (m)
bree-yah(n)

brillante (f)
bree-yahnt

ship (n)
un navire
na-veer

shirt (n)
une chemise
shuh-meez

shoe (n)
une chaussure
shoh-soor

shop (n)
un magasin
ma-ga-za(n)

shop assistant (n)
un vendeur
vahn-duhr

une vendeuse
vahn-duhz

shopper (n)
un acheteur
ash-tuhr

une acheteuse
ash-tuhz

shopping (n)
les courses
koorss

shopping bag (n)
un sac
sak

shopping list (n)
une liste de courses
leest duh koorss

short (adj)
court (m) courte (f)
koor/koort

shorts (n)
un short
short

shoulder (n)
une épaule
ay-pohl

show (n)
un spectacle
spek-ta-kluh

shower (n)
une douche
doosh

shy (adj)
timide
tee-meed

sick (adj)
malade
ma-lad

sign (n)
un panneau
pan-noh

wool
la laine

sheep
le mouton

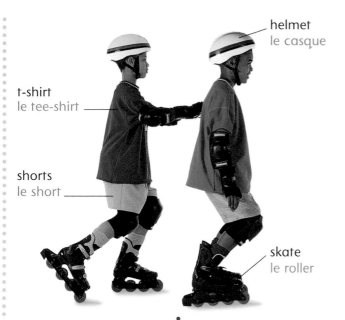

t-shirt
le tee-shirt

shorts
le short

helmet
le casque

skate
le roller

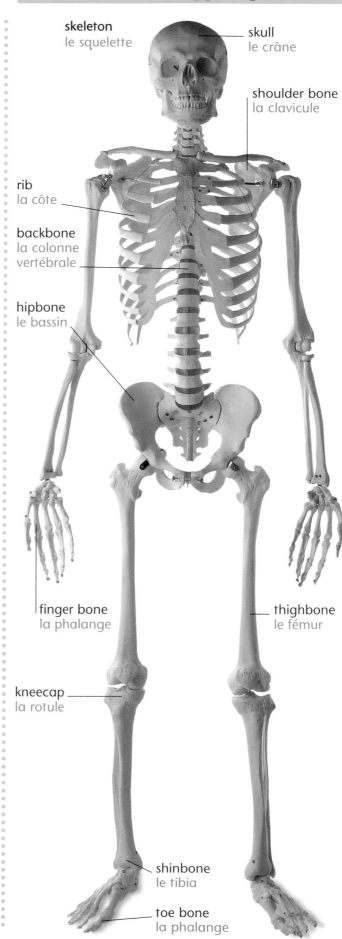

skeleton
le squelette

skull
le crâne

shoulder bone
la clavicule

rib
la côte

backbone
la colonne
vertébrale

hipbone
le bassin

finger bone
la phalange

thighbone
le fémur

kneecap
la rotule

shinbone
le tibia

toe bone
la phalange

silver (n)
l'argent (m)
lar-zhah(n)

simple (adj)
simple
sam-pluh

singing (n)
le chant
shah(n)

sink (n)
un évier
ayv-yay

sister (n)
une sœur
suhr

size (n)
la taille
tah-ye

skate (n)
un roller
ro-lair

skateboard (n)
un skate-board
skate-board

skeleton (n)
un squelette
skuh-let

skiing (n)
le ski
skee

skin (n)
la peau
poh

skipping rope (n)
une corde à sauter
kord ah soh-tay

skirt (n)
une jupe
zhewp

sky (n)
le ciel
syel

skyscraper (n)
un gratte-ciel
grat-syel

sledge (n)
une luge
lewzh

sleeping bag (n)
un sac de couchage
sak duh koosh-azh

sleeve (n)
une manche
mahnsh

sleigh (n)
un traîneau
treh-noh

slipper (n)
une pantoufle
pahn-too-fluh

A B C D E F G H I J K L M N O P Q R **S** T U V W X Y Z

snake
le serpent

tail
la queue

head
la tête

snail
l'escargot

slow (adj)
lent (m) lente (f)
lah(n)/lahnt

slowly (adv)
lentement
lahn-tuh-mah(n)

small (adj)
petit (m) petite (f)
puh-tee/puh-teet

smart (adj)
élégant (m)
ay-lay-gah(n)

élégante (f)
ay-lay-gahnt

smell (n)
une odeur
o-duhr

smoke (n)
la fumée
few-may

smooth (adj)
lisse
leess

snail (n)
un escargot
es-kar-goh

snake (n)
un serpent
sair-pah(n)

snow (n)
la neige
nehzh

snowball (n)
une boule de neige
bool duh nehzh

snowboard (n)
un snow-board
snow-board

snowflake (n)
un flocon de neige
flo-ko(n) duh nehzh

snowman (n)
un bonhomme
de neige
bon-om duh nehzh

soap (n)
le savon
sa-vo(n)

sock (n)
une chaussette
shoh-set

sofa (n)
un canapé
ka-na-pay

soft (adj)
doux (m) douce (f)
doo/dooss

soil (n)
la terre
tair

soldier (n)
un soldat
sol-da

solid (n)
un solide
sol-eed

some (adj)
quelques
kel-kuh

someone (pron)
quelqu'un
kel-ka(n)

something (pron)
quelque chose
kel-kuh shohz

sometimes (adv)
quelquefois
kel-kuh fwa

soon (adv)
bientôt
byan-toh

south (n)
le sud
sood

souvenir (n)
un souvenir
soov-neer

space (n)
l'espace (m)
less-pass

space rocket (n)
une fusée
few-zay

spade (n)
une pelle
pel

spaghetti (n)
les spaghettis
spa-get-ee

Spanish (n)
l'espagnol (m)
le-span-yol

special (adj)
particulier (m)
par-tee-kewl-yay

particulière (f)
par-tee-kewl-yair

speech (n)
un discours
dee-skoor

spider (n)
une araignée
ar-ehn-yay

sponge (n)
une éponge
ay-ponzh

spoon (n)
une cuillère
kwee-yehr

sport (n)
un sport
spor

spots (n)
les taches
tash

spring (season) (n)
le printemps
pran-tah(m)

square (n)
un carré
kar-ray

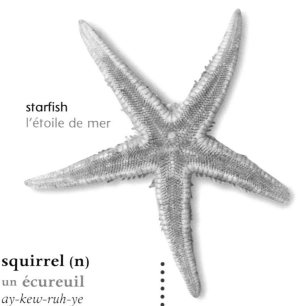

starfish
l'étoile de mer

squirrel (n)
un écureuil
ay-kew-ruh-ye

stairs (n)
un escalier
es-kal-yay

stamp (n)
un timbre
tam-bruh

star (n)
une étoile
ay-twal

starfish (n)
une étoile de mer
ay-twal duh mair

station (n)
une gare
gar

steam (n)
la buée
bway

steep (adj)
raide
rehd

stem (n)
une tige
teezh

step (n)
un pas
pa

stepfather (n)
un beau-père
boh-pair

stepmother (n)
une belle-mère
bel-mair

stick (n)
un bâton
bah-to(n)

sticker (n)
un autocollant
oh-to-ko-lah(n)

sticky (adj)
collant (m)
ko-lah(n)
collante (f)
ko-lahnt

still (adj)
immobile
im-mob-eel

stocking (n)
un bas
bah

stomach (n)
un estomac
es-to-ma

stone (n)
une pierre
pyair

storey (n)
un étage
ay-tazh

stormy (adj)
orageux (m)
or-azh-uh
orageuse (f)
or-azh-uhz

story (n)
une histoire
eest-wahr

straight (adj)
droit (m) droite (f)
drwa/drwat

strange (adj)
étrange
ay-trahnzh

straw (n)
la paille
pah-ye

strawberry (n)
une fraise
frehz

street (n)
une rue
rew

street light (n)
un réverbère
ray-vair-bair

strict (adj)
sévère
say-vehr

string (n)
une ficelle
fee-sel

stripes (n)
les rayures
ray-ewr

strong (adj)
fort (m) forte (f)
for/fort

strawberry
la fraise

student (n)
un/une élève
ay-lehv

stupid (adj)
stupide
stoo-peed

subject (n)
un sujet
soo-zhay

submarine (n)
un sous-marin
soo-ma-ra(n)

**subway
(underground) (n)**
un métro
may-troh

suddenly (adv)
tout à coup
toot ah koo

sugar (n)
le sucre
soo-kruh

suit (n)
un costume
kos-tewm

suitcase (n)
une valise
val-eez

summer (n)
l'été (m)
lay-tay

sun (n)
le soleil
so-laye

sunflower
le tournesol

A B C D E F G H I J K L M N O P Q R **S** T U V W X Y Z

suncream (n)
la **crème solaire**
krehm so-lair

sunflower (n)
un **tournesol**
toor-nuh-sol

sunglasses (n)
les **lunettes**
de soleil
lew-net duh so-laye

sunhat (n)
un **chapeau**
sha-poh

sunny (adj)
ensoleillé (m)
ensoleillée (f)
ahn-so-lay-yay

sunset (n)
un **coucher de soleil**
koo-shay duh so-laye

supermarket (n)
un **supermarché**
soo-pair-mar-shay

sure (adj)
sûr (m) sûre (f)
soor

surface (n)
une **surface**
soor-fass

surfboard (n)
une **planche de surf**
plahnsh duh surf

surfing (n)
le **surf**
surf

surgery (place) (n)
un **cabinet médical**
ka-bee-nay may-dee-kal

surprise (n)
une **surprise**
soor-preez

surprising (adj)
étonnant (m)
ay-ton-nah(n)
étonnante (f)
ay-ton-nahnt

swan (n)
un **cygne**
seen-ye

sweater (n)
un **pull**
pewl

sweet (n)
un **bonbon**
bo(n)-bʋ(n)

swimming (n)
la **natation**
na-ta-syo(n)

swimming pool (n)
une **piscine**
pee-seen

swimsuit (n)
un **maillot de bain**
ma-yoh duh ba(n)

swing (n)
une **balançoire**
ba-lahn-swahr

swing
la balançoire

T

tadpole
le têtard

table (n)
une **table**
tab-luh

table tennis (n)
le **tennis de table**
ten-neess duh tab-luh

tadpole (n)
un **têtard**
teh-tar

tail (n)
une **queue**
kuh

tall (adj)
grand (m)
grah(n)
grande (f)
grahnd

tap (n)
un **robinet**
ro-bee-nay

tape measure (n)
un **mètre**
meh-truh

taxi (n)
un **taxi**
tak-see

taxi
le taxi

tea (n)
le **thé**
tay

teacher (n)
un **maître**
meh-truh
une **maîtresse**
meh-tress

team (n)
une **équipe**
ay-keep

tea towel (n)
un **torchon**
tor-sho(n)

teddy bear (n)
un **ours en peluche**
oorss ah(n) puh-lewsh

telescope (n)
un **télescope**
tay-leh-skop

television (n)
une **télévision**
tay-lay-vee-zyo(n)

tennis (n)
le **tennis**
ten-neess

tent (n)
une **tente**
tahnt

term (n)
un **mot**
moh

terrible (adj)
terrible
tair-ee-bluh

text message (n)
un **texto**
teks-toh

that one (pron)
celui-là
suhl-wee-la

the (article)
le (m) la (f) l' (vowel)
luh/la/l

their (adj)
leur (m/f)
luhr

then (conj)
alors
al-or

there (adv)
là
la

thermometer (n)
un thermomètre
tair-mo-meh-truh

they (pron)
ils (m) elles (f)
eel/el

thick (adj)
épais (m) épaisse (f)
ay-pay/ay-pehss

thin (adj)
fin (m) fine (f)
fa(n)/feen

thing (n)
une chose
shohz

third (adj)
troisième
trwaz-yehm

thirsty (adj)
assoiffé (m)
assoiffée (f)
a-swa-fay

this one (pron)
celui-ci
suhl-wee-see

thousand
mille
meel

through (prep)
à travers
ah tra-vair

thumb (n)
un pouce
pooss

thunderstorm (n)
un orage
or-azh

ticket (n)
un billet
bee-yay

tide (n)
la marée
ma-ray

tie (n)
une cravate
kra-vat

tiger (n)
un tigre
tee-gruh

tight (adj)
serré (m) serrée (f)
sair-ray

tights (n)
les collants
ko-lah(n)

**till
(cash register) (n)**
une caisse
kess

time (n)
l'heure (f)
luhr

timetable (n)
un horaire
or-air

toad
le crapaud

tongue
la langue

tiny (adj)
minuscule
mee-new-skewl

tired (adj)
fatigué (m)
fatiguée (f)
fa-tee-gay

tissues (n)
les mouchoirs
en papier
*moosh-wahrs
ah(n) pap-yay*

toad (n)
un crapaud
kra-poh

toaster (n)
un grille-pain
gree-ye-pa(n)

today (adv)
aujourd'hui
oh-zhoor-dwee

toe (n)
un orteil
or-teye

together (adv)
ensemble
ahn-sahm-bluh

toilet (n)
les toilettes
twa-let

toilet paper (n)
le papier toilette
pap-yay twa-let

tomato (n)
une tomate
tom-at

whiskers
les
moustaches

stripes
les rayures

tail
la queue

tiger
le tigre

A
B
C
D
E
F
G
H
I
J
K
L
M
N
O
P
Q
R
S
T
U
V
W
X
Y
Z

toothbrush
la brosse à dents

tomorrow (adv)
demain
duh-ma(n)

tongue (n)
une langue
lahn-guh

tonight (adv)
cette nuit
set nwee

too (adv)
aussi
oh-see

tool (n)
un outil
oo-tee

tooth (n)
une dent
dah(n)

toothbrush (n)
une brosse à dents
bros ah dah(n)

toothpaste (n)
le dentifrice
dahn-tee-freess

top (n)
le haut
oh

torch (n)
une lampe de poche
lahmp duh posh

tortoise
la tortue

tornado (n)
une tornade
tor-nad

tortoise (n)
une tortue
tor-tew

toucan (n)
un toucan
too-kah(n)

tough (adj)
dur (m) dure (f)
dewr

tourist (n)
un/une touriste
too-reest

towards (prep)
vers
vair

towel (n)
une serviette
sair-vee-et

town (n)
une ville
veel

toy (n)
un jouet
zhoo-way

toy box (n)
un coffre à jouets
kof-fruh ah zhoo-way

toy bricks (n)
les cubes
kewb

tractor (n)
un tracteur
trak-tuhr

traffic (n)
la circulation
seer-kew-lah-syo(n)

traffic lights (n)
les feux
de signalisation
*fuh duh
seen-ya-lee-za-syo(n)*

traffic lights
les feux de signalisation

train (n)
un train
tra(n)

trainers (n)
les baskets
bas-ket

train set (toy) (n)
un train
tra(n)

transport (n)
le transport
trahn-spor

tray (n)
un plateau
pla-toh

tree (n)
un arbre
ar-bruh

trunk
la trompe

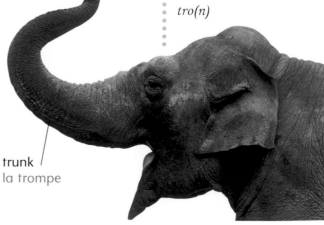

triangle (n)
un triangle
tree-yahn-gluh

trip (n)
un voyage
vwa-yazh

**trolley
(supermarket) (n)**
un caddie
ka-dee

tropical (adj)
tropical (m)
tropicale (f)
tro-pee-kal

trouble (n)
un ennui
ahn-wee

trousers (n)
un pantalon
pahn-ta-lo(n)

trowel (n)
un déplantoir
day-plahnt-wahr

truck (n)
un camion
kam-yo(n)

true (adj)
vrai (m) vraie (f)
vray

trunk (animal) (n)
une trompe
tromp

trunk (tree) (n)
un tronc
tro(n)

turkey
le dindon

U

trunks (n)
un **maillot de bain**
ma-yoh duh ba(n)

T-shirt (n)
un **tee-shirt**
tee-shirt

tube (n)
un **tube**
tewb

tummy (n)
un **ventre**
vahn-truh

tunnel (n)
un **tunnel**
tew-nel

turkey (n)
un **dindon**
dan-do(n)

turn (bend) (n)
un **tournant**
toor-nah(n)

turtle (n)
une **tortue de mer**
tor-tew duh mair

twice (adv)
deux fois
duh fwa

twin (n)
un **jumeau**
zhew-moh

une **jumelle**
zhew-mel

tyre (n)
un **pneu**
p-nuh

ugly (adj)
laid (m) laide (f)
lay/lehd

umbrella (rain) (n)
un **parapluie**
pa-ra-plwee

umbrella (sun) (n)
un **parasol**
pa-ra-sol

uncle (n)
un **oncle**
onk-luh

under (prep)
sous
soo

underwear (n)
les **sous-vêtements**
soo-veht-mah(n)

unfair (adj)
injuste
an-zhewst

uniform (n)
un **uniforme**
ew-nee-form

universe (n)
un **univers**
ew-nee-vair

uniform
l'uniforme

until (prep)
jusqu'à
zhew-ska

unusual (adj)
inhabituel (m)
inhabituelle (f)
een-ab-ee-tew-el

upside down (adv)
à l'envers
ah lahn-vair

upstairs (adv)
en haut
ah(n) oh

useful (adj)
utile
ew-teel

usually (adv)
d'habitude
da-bee-tewd

umbrella
le parapluie

V

van (n)
une **camionnette**
kam-yon-net

vegetable (n)
un **légume**
lay-gewm

vegetarian (n)
un **végétarien**
vay-zhay-ta-rya(n)

une **végétarienne**
vay-zhay-ta-ryen

verb (n)
un **verbe**
vairb

very (adv)
très
treh

vet (n)
un/une **vétérinaire**
vay-tair-ee-nair

video game (n)
un **jeu vidéo**
zhuh vee day-oh

video player (n)
un **magnétoscope**
man-yay-to-skop

village (n)
un **village**
vee-lazh

violin (n)
un **violon**
vyo-lo(n)

violin
le violon

A B C D E F G H I J K L M N O P Q R S **T U V** W X Y Z

A
B
C
D
E
F
G
H
I
J
K
L
M
N
O
P
Q
R
S
T
U
V
W
X
Y
Z

watering can
l'arrosoir

waist (n)
la taille
tah-ye

waiter (n)
un garçon de café
gar-so(n) duh ka-fay

waitress (n)
une serveuse
sair-vuhz

walk (n)
une promenade
pro-muh-nad

wall (n)
un mur
mewr

war (n)
une guerre
gair

wardrobe (n)
une armoire
arm-wahr

warm (adj)
chaud (m)
chaude (f)
shoh/shohd

warning (n)
un avertissement
av-air-tee-smah(n)

washbasin (n)
un lavabo
la-va-boh

washing machine (n)
une machine à laver
ma-sheen ah la-vay

washing-up (n)
la vaisselle
vay-sel

wasp (n)
une guêpe
gehp

watch (n)
une montre
mon-truh

water (n)
l'eau (f)
loh

watering can (n)
un arrosoir
ar-rohz-wahr

water lily (n)
un nénuphar
nay-new-far

watermelon (n)
une pastèque
pas-tehk

wave (n)
une vague
vag

way in (n)
l'entrée (f)
lahn-tray

way out (n)
la sortie
sor-tee

we (pron)
nous
noo

weak (adj)
faible
fay-bluh

weather (n)
le temps
tah(n)

website (n)
un site web
seet web

weed (n)
une mauvaise herbe
moh-vayz airb

week (n)
une semaine
suh-mehn

weekend (n)
un week-end
week-end

welcome (adj)
bienvenu (m)
bienvenue (f)
byan-vuh-new

well (adj)
bien
bya(n)

west (n)
l'ouest (m)
lwest

wet (adj)
mouillé (m)
mouillée (f)
moo-yay

whale (n)
une baleine
ba-len

wheat (n)
le blé
blay

wheel (n)
une roue
roo

wheelbarrow (n)
une brouette
broo-et

wheelchair (n)
un fauteuil roulant
foh-tuh-ye roo-lah(n)

when (adv)
quand
kah(n)

where (adv)
où
oo

while (conj)
pendant que
pahn-dah(n) kuh

whisker (n)
une moustache
moo-stash

whistle (n)
un sifflement
see-fluh-mah(n)

wave
la vague

wing
l'aile

white (adj)
blanc (m)
blanche (f)
blah(n)/blahnsh

who (pron)
qui
kee

why (adv)
pourquoi
poor-kwa

wide (adj)
large
larzh

wife (n)
une épouse
ay-pooz

wind (n)
le vent
vah(n)

window (n)
une fenêtre
fuh-neh-truh

windy (adj)
il y a du vent
eel ya dew vah(n)

wing (n)
une aile
ehl

winner (n)
un gagnant
gan-yah(n)

une gagnante
gan-yahnt

winter (n)
l'hiver (m)
lee-vair

with (prep)
avec
av-ek

without (prep)
sans
sah(n)

wolf (n)
un loup
loo

woman (n)
une femme
fam

wood (n)
le bois
bwa

wooden (adj)
en bois
ah(n) bwa

wool (n)
la laine
lehn

woolly hat (n)
un bonnet
bon-nay

word (n)
un mot
moh

world (n)
un monde
mond

worm (n)
un ver
vair

worst (adj)
pire
peer

writing (act of) (n)
l'écriture (f)
lay-kree-tewr

Y

yacht
le yacht

yacht
le yacht

yacht (n)
un yacht
yoht

year (n)
une année
un an (for numbers)
an-nay/ah(n)

yellow (adj)
jaune
zhohn

yesterday (adv)
hier
yair

yoghurt (n)
un yaourt
ya-oort

you (pron)
tu/vous
tew/voo

young (adj)
jeune
zhuhn

your (adj)
votre (m/f)
vo-truh

Z

zebra
le zèbre

zebra
le zèbre

zebra (n)
un zèbre
zeh-bruh

zebra crossing (n)
un passage clouté
pa-sazh kloo-tay

zip (n)
une fermeture
éclair
fair-muh-tewr ay-klair

zone (n)
une zone
zohn

zoo (n)
un zoo
zoh

zip
la fermeture éclair

A B C D E F G H I J K L M N O P Q R S T U V **W** X **Y** **Z**

French A–Z

In this section, French words are in alphabetical order. They are followed by the English translation and a few letters to show what type of word it is – a noun (n) or adjective (adj), for example. Look at p56 to see a list of the different types of words.

Nouns in French are either masculine or feminine. We have used (m) and (f) to tell you which they are. Sometimes a word in French might mean more than one thing in English, so there might be two translations underneath.

Most of the nouns (naming words) here are singular (only one of the object). To make a noun plural (for more than one thing) you usually just add an "s" – the same as in English. In French though, the other words in the sentence change too – *le* and *la* become *les*. The adjectives also change, usually getting an extra "s" at the end.

à l'arrière (adv)
back (opposite of front)

à l'envers (adv)
upside down

à l'intérieur de (prep)
inside

à la mode (adv)
fashionable

à travers (prep)
through

abeille (n) (f)
bee

absent/absente (adj)
away

accident (n) (m)
accident

acheteur/acheteuse (n) (m/f)
shopper

activité (n) (f)
activity

addition (n) (f)
bill

adorable (adj)
lovely

adresse (n) (f)
address

adresse électronique (n) (f)
email address

adulte (n) (m/f)
adult

aéroport (n) (m)
airport

affaires (n) (f)
business

affamé/affamée (adj)
hungry

affiche (n) (f)
poster

âge (n) (m)
age

agneau (n) (m)
lamb

aide (n) (f)
help

aïe !
ouch!

aigle (n) (m)
eagle

aigu/aiguë (adj)
sharp

aiguille (n) (f)
needle

aile (n) (f)
wing

aimant (n) (m)
magnet

air (n) (m)
air

algue (n) (f)
seaweed

alligator (n) (m)
alligator

alors (conj)
then

alphabet (n) (m)
alphabet

ambulance (n) (f)
ambulance

ami/amie (n) (m/f)
friend

amical/amicale (adj)
friendly

ample (adj)
loose

ampoule (n) (f)
bulb (light)

amusement (n) (m)
fun

ananas (n) (m)
pineapple

ancre (n) (f)
anchor

anglais (n) (m)
English

animal (n) (m)
animal

animal familier (n) (m)
pet

année/an (n) (f/m)
year

anniversaire (n) (m)
birthday

antenne (n) (f)
antenna

appareil photo (n) (m)
camera

apparence (n) (f)
appearance

appartement (n) (m)
flat (apartment)

après (prep)
after, past

après-midi (n) (m)
afternoon

araignée (n) (f)
spider

arbre (n) (m)
tree

arc-en-ciel (n) (m)
rainbow

arche (n) (f)
arch

argent (n) (m)
money, silver

argent de poche (n) (m)
pocket money

armée (n) (f)
army

armoire (n) (f)
wardrobe

arrêt de bus (n) (m)
bus stop

arrivée (n) (f)
arrival

arrosoir (n) (m)
watering can

art (n) (m)
art

artiste (n) (m/f)
artist

ascenseur (n) (m)
lift

assez (adv)
enough

assiette (n) (f)
plate

assistant/assistante (n) (m/f)
assistant

assoiffé/assoiffée (adj)
thirsty

astronaute (n) (m/f)
astronaut

astronome (n) (m/f)
astronomer

athlétisme (n) (m)
athletics

atlas (n) (m)
atlas

au rez-de-chaussée (adv)
downstairs

au-dessous de (prep)
below

au-dessus de (prep)
above

aujourd'hui (adv)
today

aussi (adv)
also, too

autobus (n) (m)
bus

autocar (n) (m)
coach

autocollant (n) (m)
sticker

automne (n) (m)
autumn

autoroute (n) (f)
motorway

autour (prep)
around

autre (adj)
other

avant (prep)
before

avec (prep)
with

avenir (n) (m)
future

aventure (n) (f)
adventure

avertissement (n) (m)
warning

avion (n) (m)
aeroplane, plane

avion à réaction (n) (m)
jet

avocat (n) (m)
avocado

B

babouin (n) (m)
baboon

badminton (n) (m)
badminton

bagages (n) (m)
luggage

bague (n) (f)
ring

baignoire (n) (f)
bath

baiser (n) (m)
kiss

balai (n) (m)
broom

balançoire (n) (f)
swing

balcon (n) (m)
balcony

baleine (n) (f)
whale

balle (n) (f)
ball

ballon (n) (m)
ball, balloon

ballon de football (n) (m)
football (ball)

banane (n) (f)
banana

banc (n) (m)
bench

bande (n) (f)
band

banque (n) (f)
bank (money)

barbe (n) (f)
beard

barbecue (n) (m)
barbecue

barrière (n) (f)
fence

bas/basse (adj)
low

bas (n) (m)
stocking

base-ball (n) (m)
baseball

basket-ball (n) (m)
basketball

baskets (n) (f)
trainers

bataille (n) (f)
battle

bateau (n) (m)
boat

bateau à voiles (n) (m)
sailing boat

bateau de pêche (n) (m)
fishing boat

bateau de sauvetage (n) (m)
lifeboat

bâtiment (n) (m)
building

bâton (n) (m)
stick

batte (n) (f)
bat (sports)

batterie (n) (f)
drum kit

beau/belle (adj)
beautiful

beaucoup (adv)
(a) lot

beau-père (n) (m)
stepfather

beauté (n) (f)
beauty

bébé (n) (m)
baby

bec (n) (m)
beak

belle-mère (n) (f)
stepmother

bête (n) (f)
creature

beurre (n) (m)
butter

bibliothèque (n) (f)
library

bidon (n) (m)
can

bien (adj)
fine

bien (adv)
well

bientôt (adv)
soon

bienvenu/bienvenue (adj)
welcome

bijou (n) (m)
jewel

bijoux (n) (m)
jewellery

billes (n) (f)
marbles (toy)

billet (n) (m)
note, ticket

biscuit (n) (m)
biscuit

blague (n) (f)
joke

blanc/blanche (adj)
white

blé (n) (m)
wheat

blessure (n) (f)
injury

bleu/bleue (adj)
blue

blond/blonde (adj)
blonde

blouson (n) (m)
jacket

bois (n) (m)
wood

boisson (n) (f)
drink

boîte (n) (f)
box

boîte aux lettres (n) (f)
letter box, postbox

boîte d'allumettes (n) (f)
matchbox

bol (n) (m)
bowl (cereal)

bon/bonne (adj)
good

bonbon (n) (m)
sweet

bonde (n) (f)
plug

bondé/bondée (adj)
crowded

bonhomme de neige (n) (m)
snowman

bon marché (adj)
cheap

bonnet (n) (m)
woolly hat

bord (n) (m)
edge

bord de la mer (n) (m)
seaside

botte (n) (f)
boot

bouche (n) (f)
mouth

boucle d'oreille (n) (f)
earring

boue (n) (f)
mud

bouée (n) (f)
buoy

boueux/boueuse (adj)
muddy

bougie (n) (f)
candle

bouilloire (n) (f)
kettle

boulangerie (n) (f)
bakery

boule de neige (n) (f)
snowball

boussole (n) (f)
compass

bouteille (n) (f)
bottle

bouton (n) (m)
button

bracelet (n) (m)
bracelet

branche (n) (f)
branch

bras (n) (m)
arm

brillant/brillante (adj)
bright, shiny

brise (n) (f)
breeze

brosse à cheveux (n) (f)
hairbrush

brosse à dents (n) (f)
toothbrush

brouette (n) (f)
wheelbarrow

brouillard (n) (m)
fog

bruyant/bruyante (adj)
loud, noisy

buée (n) (f)
steam

buisson (n) (m)
bush

bulbe (n) (m)
bulb (plant)

bulle (n) (f)
bubble

bureau (n) (m)
desk, office

bureau de poste (n) (m)
post office

but (n) (m)
goal

C

c'est
it's (it is)

cabane (n) (f)
hut

cabinet médical (n) (m)
surgery (place)

cacahuète (n) (f)
peanut

cache-cache (n) (m)
hide-and-seek

caddie (n) (m)
trolley (supermarket)

cadeau (n) (m)
present

cadre (n) (m)
frame

café (n) (m)
café, coffee

cage (n) (f)
cage

cahier (n) (m)
exercise book

caisse (n) (f)
checkout, till

calculatrice (n) (f)
calculator

calendrier (n) (m)
calendar

calme (adj)
calm

camarade (n) (m/f)
partner

camion (n) (m)
lorry, truck

camion de pompier (n) (m)
fire engine

camionnette (n) (f)
van

campagne (n) (f)
countryside

canapé (n) (m)
sofa

canard (n) (m)
duck

caneton (n) (m)
duckling

canoë (n) (m)
canoe

canot (n) (m)
rowing boat

cape (n) (f)
cloak

capitale (n) (f)
capital

capuche (n) (f)
hood

carburant (n) (m)
fuel

carnet (n) (m)
notebook

carotte (n) (f)
carrot

carré (n) (m)
square

carrefour (n) (m)
crossing

cartable (n) (m)
school bag

carte (n) (f)
card, map, menu

carte d'anniversaire (n) (f)
birthday card

carte postale (n) (f)
postcard

cartes (n) (f)
cards

carton (n) (m)
cardboard

casque (n) (m)
helmet

casquette (n) (f)
cap

cassé/cassée (adj)
broken

casserole (n) (f)
saucepan

cassette (n) (f)
cassette

cave (n) (f)
cellar

CD (n) (m)
CD

ceinture (n) (f)
belt

célèbre (adj)
famous

celui-ci (pron)
this one

celui-là (pron)
that one

centre (n) (m)
centre

cercle (n) (m)
circle

céréale (n) (f)
cereal

cerf-volant (n) (m)
kite

certain/certaine (adj)
certain

cerveau (n) (m)
brain

cette nuit
tonight

chaîne (n) (f)
chain

chaise (n) (f)
chair

chaise longue (n) (f)
deck chair

chaleur (n) (f)
heat

chambre (n) (f)
bedroom

chameau (n) (m)
camel

champ (n) (m)
field

champignon (n) (m)
mushroom

chanceux/chanceuse (adj)
lucky

changement (n) (m)
change

chant (n) (m)
singing

chapeau (n) (m)
hat, sunhat

chaque (adj)
each

charrette (n) (f)
cart

chat (n) (m)
cat

château de sable (n) (m)
sandcastle

chaton (n) (m)
kitten

chaud/chaude (adj)
hot, warm

chaussette (n) (f)
sock

chaussure (n) (f)
shoe

chauve-souris (n) (f)
bat (animal)

chef (n) (m/f)
chef

chemin (n) (m)
path

cheminée (n) (f)
chimney

chemise (n) (f)
shirt

chemisier (n) (m)
blouse

chenille (n) (f)
caterpillar

cher/chère (adj)
dear (special, expensive)

cheval (n) (m)
horse

chevalier (n) (m)
knight

cheveux (n) (m)
hair

cheville (n) (f)
ankle

chèvre (n) (f)
goat

chewing-gum (n) (m)
chewing gum

chien (n) (m)
dog

chien de berger (n) (m)
sheepdog

chimpanzé (n) (m)
chimpanzee

chiot (n) (m)
puppy

chirurgie (n) (f)
surgery (operation)

chocolat (n) (m)
chocolate

chocolat chaud (n) (m)
hot chocolate

chose (n) (f)
thing

chou (n) (m)
cabbage

ciel (n) (m)
sky

cil (n) (m)
eyelash

cinéma (n) (m)
cinema

cintre (n) (m)
coat hanger

circulation (n) (f)
traffic

cirque (n) (m)
circus

ciseaux (n) (m)
scissors

citron (n) (m)
lemon

citrouille (n) (f)
pumpkin

clair/claire (adj)
clear, light

clavier (n) (m)
keyboard

clé (n) (f)
key

client/cliente (n) (m/f)
customer

cloche (n) (f)
bell

clown (n) (m)
clown

coccinelle (n) (f)
ladybird

cochon (n) (m)
pig

cochon d'Inde (n) (m)
guinea pig

code postal (n) (m)
postcode

cœur (n) (m)
heart

coffre à jouets (n) (m)
toy box

coiffeur/coiffeuse (n) (m/f)
hairdresser's

coin (n) (m)
corner

collant/collante (adj)
sticky

collants (n) (m)
tights

colle (n) (f)
glue

collier (n) (m)
collar, necklace

colline (n) (f)
hill

coloré/colorée (adj)
colourful

comique (n) (m)
comic

commandes (n) (f)
controls

comme (prep)
like

comment (adv)
how

commode (n) (f)
chest of drawers

concert (n) (m)
concert

confiture (n) (f)
jam

confortable (adj)
comfortable

congélateur (n) (m)
freezer

content/contente (adj)
happy

continent (n) (m)
continent

contraire (n) (m)
opposite

coquillage (n) (m)
shell

corde (n) (f)
rope

corde à sauter (n) (f)
skipping rope

corne (n) (f)
horn

corps (n) (m)
body

costume (n) (m)
costume, suit

côte (n) (f)
coast

coton (n) (m)
cotton

cou (n) (m)
neck

coucher de soleil (n) (m)
sunset

coude (n) (m)
elbow

couette (n) (f)
duvet

couleur (n) (f)
colour

couloir (n) (m)
hall

cour de récréation (n) (f)
playground

courageux/courageuse (adj)
brave

courbe (adj)
curved

couronne (n) (f)
crown

course (n) (f)
race

course à pied (n) (f)
running

courses (n) (f)
shopping

court/courte (adj)
short

cousin/cousine (n) (m/f)
cousin

coussin (n) (m)
cushion

couteau (n) (m)
knife

couvercle (n) (m)
lid

couverture (n) (f)
blanket

cow-boy (n) (m)
cowboy

crabe (n) (m)
crab

crapaud (n) (m)
toad

cravate (n) (f)
tie

crayon à papier (n) (m)
pencil

crayon de couleur (n) (m)
coloured pencil, crayon

crèche (n) (f)
nursery

crème (n) (f)
cream

crème solaire (n) (f)
suncream

crêpe (n) (f)
pancake

crocodile (n) (m)
crocodile

cruche (n) (f)
jug

cube (n) (m)
cube

cubes (n) (m)
toy bricks

cuillère (n) (f)
spoon

cuisine (n) (f)
kitchen

cuisinière (n) (f)
cooker

curieux/curieuse (adj)
curious

cygne (n) (m)
swan

D

d'abord (adv)
first

d'habitude (adv)
usually

daim (n) (m)
deer

danger (n) (m)
danger

dangereux/dangereuse (adj)
dangerous

dans (prep)
into

danseur/danseuse (n) (m/f)
dancer

danseur/danseuse classique (n) (m/f)
ballet dancer

date (n) (f)
date

dauphin (n) (m)
dolphin

de (prep)
from

de l'autre côté de (prep)
across

dé/dés (n) (m)
dice

décoration (n) (f)
decoration

défi (n) (m)
challenge

défilé (n) (m)
parade

déguisement (n) (m)
fancy dress

dehors (adv)
outside

déjà (adv)
already

déjeuner (n) (m)
lunch

délicieux/délicieuse (adj)
delicious

deltaplane (n) (m)
hang-glider

demain (adv)
tomorrow

demi-cercle (n) (m)
semicircle

dent (n) (f)
tooth

dentifrice (n) (m)
toothpaste

dentiste (n) (m/f)
dentist

déplantoir (n) (m)
trowel

dernier/dernière (adj)
last

derrière (prep)
behind

désert (n) (m)
desert

désordre (n) (m)
mess

dessert (n) (m)
dessert, pudding

dessin (n) (m)
drawing (act of)

deux fois
twice

deuxième (adj)
second (2nd)

devoirs (n) (m)
homework

diagramme (n) (m)
diagram

dictionnaire (n) (m)
dictionary

Dieu (n) (m)
God

différent/différente (adj)
different

difficile (adj)
difficult

digital/digitale (adj)
digital

dindon (n) (m)
turkey

dîner (n) (m)
dinner

dinosaure (n) (m)
dinosaur

directement (adv)
directly

direction (n) (f)
direction

discothèque (n) (f)
disco

discours (n) (m)
speech

disque dur (n) (m)
hard drive

distance (n) (f)
distance

divorcé/divorcée (adj)
divorced

doigt (n) (m)
finger

dôme (n) (m)
dome

dos (n) (m)
back (body)

doucement (adv)
gently

douche (n) (f)
shower

doux/douce (adj)
gentle, soft

dragon (n) (m)
dragon

drap (n) (m)
sheet

drapeau (n) (m)
flag

droit/droite (adj)
straight, right (not left)

dur/dure (adj)
hard, tough

DVD (n) (m)
DVD

E

eau (n) (f)
water

échange (n) (m)
exchange

écharpe (n) (f)
scarf

échecs (n) (m)
chess

échelle (n) (f)
ladder

écho (n) (m)
echo

éclair (n) (m)
lightning

école (n) (f)
school

écran (n) (m)
screen

écriture (n) (f)
writing (act of)

écureuil (n) (m)
squirrel

effet (n) (m)
effect

effrayé/effrayée (adj)
frightened

égal/égale (adj)
equal

église (n) (f)
church

élastique (n) (m)
rubber band

électrique (adj)
electrical

élégant/élégante (adj)
smart

éléphant (n) (m)
elephant

élève (n) (m/f)
pupil, student

elle (pron)
she

elles (pron)
they

e-mail (n) (m)
email

émission (n) (f)
programme (TV)

emploi (n) (m)
job

en arrière (adv)
backwards

en avant (adv)
forward

en bois
wooden

en bonne santé
healthy

en colère
angry

en cuir
leather

en espèces
(in) cash

en face de (prep)
opposite

en forme
fit

en haut (adv)
upstairs

en plastique
plastic

en retard
late

en sécurité
safe

encore (adv)
again

encre (n) (f)
ink

encyclopédie (n) (f)
encyclopedia

endroit (n) (m)
place

enfant/enfants (n) (m/f)
child/children

ennui (n) (m)
trouble

ennuyeux/ennuyeuse (adj)
boring

ensemble (adv)
together

ensoleillé/ensoleillée (adj)
sunny

enthousiaste (adj)
enthusiastic

entre (prep)
between

entrée (n) (f)
entrance, way in

enveloppe (n) (f)
envelope

environ (adv)
about

environnement (n) (m)
environment

épais/épaisse (adj)
thick

épaule (n) (f)
shoulder

éponge (n) (f)
sponge

épouse (n) (f)
wife

épuisette (n) (f)
net

équateur (n) (m)
equator

équipage (n) (m)
crew

équipe (n) (f)
team

équitation (n) (f)
horse riding, riding

erreur (n) (f)
mistake

escalier (n) (m)
stairs

escargot (n) (m)
snail

espace (n) (m)
space

espagnol (n) (m)
Spanish

esquimau (n) (m)
ice lolly

essence (n) (f)
petrol

essuie-tout (n) (m)
paper towel

est (n) (m)
east

estomac (n) (m)
stomach

et (conj)
and

étage (n) (m)
storey

étagère (n) (f)
shelf

étang (n) (m)
pond

été (n) (m)
summer

éteint/éteinte (adj)
extinct

étoile (n) (f)
star

étoile de mer (n) (f)
starfish

étonnant/étonnante (adj)
surprising

étrange (adj)
strange

étranger/étrangère (adj)
foreign

être humain (n) (m)
human

étroit/étroite (adj)
narrow

événement (n) (m)
event

évier (n) (m)
sink

exact/exacte (adj)
right (correct)

examen (n) (m)
exam

excellent/excellente (adj)
excellent

excité/excitée (adj)
excited

exercice (n) (m)
exercise

expédition (n) (f)
expedition

expérience (n) (f)
experiment

expert/experte (n) (m/f)
expert

explorateur/exploratrice (n) (m/f)
explorer

explosion (n) (f)
explosion

exposé (n) (m)
report (for school)

extrêmement (adv)
extremely

F

fabuleux/fabuleuse (adj)
fabulous

facile (adj)
easy

facteur/factrice (n) (m/f)
postman

faible (adj)
faint (pale), weak

fait (n) (m)
fact

falaise (n) (f)
cliff

famille (n) (f)
family

fantastique (adj)
fantastic

farine (n) (f)
flour

fatigué/fatiguée (adj)
tired

faucon (n) (m)
hawk

fauteuil (n) (m)
armchair

fauteuil roulant (n) (m)
wheelchair

faux/fausse (adj)
false

femme (n) (f)
female (human), woman

fenêtre (n) (f)
window

fer à repasser (n) (m)
iron (clothes)

ferme (n) (f)
farm

fermé/fermée (adj)
closed

fermeture éclair (n) (f)
zip

fermier/fermière (n) (m/f)
farmer

ferry-boat (n) (m)
ferry

fête (n) (f)
festival, party

feu (n) (m)
fire

feuille (n) (f)
leaf

feutre (n) (m)
felt-tip pen

feux de signalisation (n) (m)
traffic lights

ficelle (n) (f)
string

fille (n) (f)
daughter, girl

film (n) (m)
film

fin (n) (f)
end (final part)

fin/fine (adj)
thin

flèche (n) (f)
arrow

fleur (n) (f)
flower

flocon de neige (n) (m)
snowflake

flûte (n) (f)
flute

foin (n) (m)
hay

foire (n) (f)
fair

fond (n) (m)
bottom

football (n) (m)
football (game)

forêt (n) (f)
forest

forêt tropicale (n) (f)
rainforest

forme (n) (f)
shape

formidable (adj)
great

fort/forte (adj)
strong

four (n) (m)
oven

fourchette (n) (f)
fork

fourmi (n) (f)
ant

frais/fraîche (adj)
cool, fresh

fraise (n) (f)
strawberry

framboise (n) (f)
raspberry

français (n) (m)
French

frère (n) (m)
brother

frisé/frisée (adj)
curly

frites (n) (f)
chips

froid/froide (adj)
cold

fromage (n) (m)
cheese

fruit (n) (m)
fruit

fruits de mer (n) (m)
seafood

fumée (n) (f)
smoke

fusée (n) (f)
rocket, space rocket

G

gagnant/gagnante (n) (m/f)
winner

galet (n) (m)
pebble

gant (n) (m)
glove

gant de cuisine (n) (m)
oven glove

garage (n) (m)
garage

garçon (n) (m)
boy

garçon de café (n) (m)
waiter

gare (n) (f)
railway station, station

gâteau (n) (m)
cake

gâteau d'anniversaire (n) (m)
birthday cake

gauche (adj)
left

gaucher/gauchère (adj)
left-handed

gaz (n) (m)
gas

géant (n) (m)
giant

genou (n) (m)
knee

gens (n) (m)
people

gentil/gentille (adj)
kind (gentle)

gilet de sauvetage (n) (m)
life jacket

girafe (n) (f)
giraffe

glace (n) (f)
ice, ice-cream

glacier (n) (m)
glacier

glaçon (n) (m)
ice cube

globe (n) (m)
globe

golf (n) (m)
golf

gomme (n) (f)
rubber (eraser)

gorille (n) (m)
gorilla

goutte (n) (f)
drop

gouvernement (n) (m)
government

graine (n) (f)
seed

grand/grande (adj)
big, tall

grand-mère (n) (f)
grandmother

grand-père (n) (m)
grandfather

grands-parents (n) (m)
grandparents

grange (n) (f)
barn

gratte-ciel (n) (m)
skyscraper

grenier (n) (m)
attic

grenouille (n) (f)
frog

griffe (n) (f)
claw

grille-pain (n) (m)
toaster

gros/grosse (adj)
big, fat

grotte (n) (f)
cave

groupe (n) (m)
group

grue (n) (f)
crane

guépard (n) (m)
cheetah

guêpe (n) (f)
wasp

guerre (n) (f)
war

guide (n) (m)
guide

guitare (n) (f)
guitar

gymnastique (n) (f)
gymnastics

H

habitat (n) (m)
habitat

hamster (n) (m)
hamster

hanche (n) (f)
hip

handicapé/handicapée (adj)
disabled

haricots blancs (n) (m)
beans

haut/haute (adj)
high

hélicoptère (n) (m)
helicopter (n)

hélicoptère de police (n) (m)
police helicopter

herbe (n) (f)
grass

héron (n) (m)
heron

héros (n) (m)
hero

heure (n) (f)
hour, time

heures d'ouverture (n) (f)
opening hours

hibou (n) (m)
owl

hier (adv)
yesterday

histoire (n) (f)
history, story

historique (adj)
historical

hiver (n) (m)
winter

hockey (n) (m)
hockey

hockey sur glace (n) (m)
ice hockey

homme (n) (m)
male (human), man

hôpital (n) (m)
hospital

horaire (n) (m)
timetable

horloge (n) (f)
clock

horrible (adj)
horrible

hors de (prep)
out of

hot-dog (n) (m)
hot dog

hôtel (n) (m)
hotel

huile (n) (f)
oil

I

idée (n) (f)
idea

il (pron)
he

il y a du vent
windy

île (n) (f)
island

ils/elles (pron)
they

image (n) (f)
picture

immobile (adj)
still

imperméable (n) (m)
raincoat

important/importante (adj)
important

impossible (adj)
impossible

incroyable (adj)
amazing

infirmière (n) (f)
nurse

information (n) (f)
information

ingrédient (n) (m)
ingredient

inhabituel/inhabituelle (adj)
unusual

injuste (adj)
unfair

inondation (n) (f)
flood

insecte (n) (m)
insect

insigne (n) (m)
badge

instruction (n) (f)
instruction

instrument (n) (m)
instrument

intelligent/intelligente (adj)
clever

intéressant/intéressante (adj)
interesting

international/ internationale (adj)
international

Internet (n) (m)
Internet

invitation (n) (f)
invitation

J

jamais (adv)
never

jambe (n) (f)
leg

jardin (n) (m)
garden

jardinier/jardinière (n) (m/f)
gardener

jaune (adj)
yellow

je/j' (pron)
I

jean (n) (m)
jeans

jeu (n) (m)
game

jeu de plateau (n) (m)
board game

jeu électronique (n) (m)
computer game

jeu vidéo (n) (m)
video game (n)

jeune (adj)
young

Jeux olympiques (n) (m)
Olympic Games

joli/jolie (adj)
pretty

jouet (n) (m)
toy

joueur/joueuse (n) (m/f)
player

jour (n) (m)
day

journal (n) (m)
diary, newspaper

judo (n) (m)
judo

jumeau/jumelle (n) (m/f)
twin

jumelles (n) (f)
binoculars

jungle (n) (f)
jungle

jupe (n) (f)
skirt

jus (n) (m)
juice

jus d'orange (n) (m)
orange juice

jusqu'à (prep)
until

juste (adj)
correct

juste (adv)
just

K

kangourou (n) (m)
kangaroo

karaté (n) (m)
karate

koala (n) (m)
koala

L

la/lui/l' (pron)
her

là (adv)
there

là-bas (adv)
over there

lac (n) (m)
lake

laid/laide (adj)
ugly

laine (n) (f)
wool

lait (n) (m)
milk

laitier/laitière (adj)
dairy

laitue (n) (f)
lettuce

lampe (n) (f)
lamp

lampe de poche (n) (f)
torch

langue (n) (f)
language, tongue

lapin (n) (m)
rabbit

large (adj)
wide

lavabo (n) (m)
washbasin

le/lui/l' (pron)
him

le/la/l'/les (article)
the

le sien/la sienne (pron)
hers / his

leçon (n) (f)
lesson

lecteur de CD (n) (m)
CD player

lecteur de DVD (n) (m)
DVD player

lecture (n) (f)
reading

léger/légère (adj)
light (not heavy)

légume (n) (m)
vegetable

lent/lente (adj)
slow

lentement (adv)
slowly

léopard (n) (m)
leopard

lettre (n) (f)
letter (alphabet, post)

leur (adj)
their

lézard (n) (m)
lizard

libellule (n) (f)
dragonfly

liberté (n) (f)
freedom

librairie (n) (f)
bookshop

lièvre (n) (m)
hare

ligne (n) (f)
line

limonade (n) (f)
lemonade

lion (n) (m)
lion

lion de mer (n) (m)
sea lion (n)

liquide (n) (m)
liquid (n)

lisse (adj)
smooth

liste (n) (f)
list

liste de courses (n) (f)
shopping list

lit (n) (m)
bed

livre (n) (m)
book

loi (n) (f)
law

loin (adv)
far

loisir (n) (m)
hobby

long/longue (adj)
long

losange (n) (m)
diamond (shape)

loup (n) (m)
wolf

loupe (n) (f)
magnifying glass

lourd/lourde (adj)
heavy

luge (n) (f)
sledge

lumière (n) (f)
light

lune (n) (f)
moon

lunettes (n) (f)
glasses

lunettes de natation (n) (f)
goggles

lunettes de soleil (n) (f)
sunglasses

M

machine (n) (f)
machine

machine à laver (n) (f)
washing machine

magasin (n) (m)
shop

magazine (n) (m)
magazine

magicien/magicienne (n) (m/f)
magician

magnétique (adj)
magnetic

magnétoscope (n) (m)
video player

maillot de bain (n) (m)
swimsuit, trunks

main (n) (f)
hand

maintenant (adv)
now

mais (conj)
but

maison (n) (f)
home, house

maître/maîtresse (n) (m/f)
teacher

mal de tête (n) (m)
headache

malade (adj)
ill, sick

maladie (n) (f)
illness

maman (n) (f)
mum

mammifère (n) (m)
mammal

manche (n) (f)
sleeve

manchot (n) (m)
penguin

manteau (n) (m)
coat

maquillage (n) (m)
make-up

marché (n) (m)
market

marée (n) (f)
tide

mari (n) (m)
husband

marié/mariée (adj)
married

marin (n) (m)
sailor

marionnette (n) (f)
puppet

marron (adj)
brown

masque (n) (m)
mask

match (n) (m)
match (football)

matériel (n) (m)
equipment

mathématiques (n) (f)
maths

matin (n) (m)
morning

mauvais/mauvaise (adj)
bad

mauvaise herbe (n) (f)
weed

me/moi/m' (pron)
me

médecin (n) (m)
doctor

médicament (n) (m)
medicine

méduse (n) (f)
jellyfish

meilleur/meilleure (adj)
better

mélange (n) (m)
mixture

melon (n) (m)
melon

même (adv)
even

même (adj)
same

menton (n) (m)
chin

mer (n) (f)
sea

mère (n) (f)
mother

message (n) (m)
message

mesure (n) (f)
measurement

mètre (n) (m)
tape measure

métro (n) (m)
subway (underground)

meubles (n) (m)
furniture

micro-ondes (n) (m)
microwave

miel (n) (m)
honey

mieux (adj)
best

milieu (n) (m)
middle

milk-shake (n) (m)
milk shake

mille
thousand

milliard
billion

million
million

minéral (n) (m)
mineral

minuit (n) (m)
midnight

minuscule (adj)
tiny

minute (n) (f)
minute

miroir (n) (m)
mirror

mitaine (n) (f)
mitten

mode (n) (f)
fashion

mois (n) (m)
month

moisson (n) (f)
harvest

moissonneuse-batteuse
(n) (f)
combine harvester

moitié (n) (f)
half

mon/ma (adj)
my

monde (n) (m)
world

monstre (n) (m)
monster

montagne (n) (f)
mountain

montgolfière (n) (f)
hot-air balloon

montre (n) (f)
watch

moquette (n) (f)
carpet

morceau (n) (m)
piece

mort/morte (adj)
dead

mosquée (n) (f)
mosque

mot (n) (m)
term, word

moteur (n) (m)
motor

motif (n) (m)
pattern

moto (n) (f)
motorbike

mouche (n) (f)
fly

mouchoir (n) (m)
handkerchief

mouchoirs en papier
(n) (m)
tissues

mouette (n) (f)
seagull

mouillé/mouillée (adj)
wet

moustache (n) (f)
moustache, whisker

mouton (n) (m)
sheep

mur (n) (m)
wall

mûr/mûre (adj)
ripe

musée (n) (m)
museum

musicien/musicienne
(n) (m/f)
musician

musique (n) (f)
music

N

n'importe qui (pron)
anybody

n'importe quoi (pron)
anything

nageoire (n) (f)
fin

natation (n) (f)
swimming

nature (n) (f)
nature

navire (n) (m)
ship

neige (n) (f)
snow

nénuphar (n) (m)
water lily

neveu (n) (m)
nephew

nez (n) (m)
nose

nid (n) (m)
nest

nièce (n) (f)
niece

Noël (n) (m)
Christmas

nœud (n) (m)
knot

noir/noire (adj)
black

nom (n) (m)
name

nombre (n) (m)
number

nord (n) (m)
north

note (n) (f)
mark

notre (adj)
our

nouilles (n) (f)
noodles

nourriture (n) (f)
food

nous (pron)
we

nouveau/nouvelle (adj)
new

nouvelles (n) (f)
news

nuage (n) (m)
cloud

nuageux/nuageuse (adj)
cloudy

nuit (n) (f)
night

nulle part (adv)
nowhere

O

objet (n) (m)
object

occupé/occupée (adj)
busy

océan (n) (m)
ocean

odeur (n) (f)
smell

œil (n) (m)
eye

œuf (n) (m)
egg

oignon (n) (m)
onion

oiseau (n) (m)
bird

oiseau-mouche (n) (m)
hummingbird

ombre (n) (f)
shadow

oncle (n) (m)
uncle

ongle (n) (m)
nail

opération (n) (f)
operation

or (n) (m)
gold

orage (n) (m)
thunderstorm

orageux/orageuse (adj)
stormy

orange (adj)
orange (colour)

orange (n) (f)
orange (fruit)

orchestre (n) (m)
orchestra

ordinateur (n) (m)
computer

ordinateur portable (n) (m)
laptop

ordures (n) (f)
rubbish

oreille (n) (f)
ear

oreiller (n) (m)
pillow

orteil (n) (m)
toe

os (n) (m)
bone

otite (n) (f)
earache

ou (conj)
or

où (adv)
where

ouest (n) (m)
west

ouragan (n) (m)
hurricane

ours (n) (m)
bear

ours blanc (n) (m)
polar bear

ours en peluche (n) (m)
teddy bear

outil (n) (m)
tool

ouvert/ouverte (adj)
open

ovale (n) (m)
oval

P

page (n) (f)
page

paille (n) (f)
drinking straw, straw

pain (n) (m)
bread

paire (n) (f)
pair

paix (n) (f)
peace

palme (n) (f)
flipper

palmier (n) (m)
palm tree

panda (n) (m)
panda

panier (n) (m)
basket

panier repas (n) (m)
lunch box

panneau (n) (m)
board (notice), sign

pantalon (n) (m)
trousers

pantoufle (n) (f)
slipper

papa (n) (m)
dad

papier (n) (m)
paper

papier toilette (n) (m)
toilet paper

papillon (n) (m)
butterfly

papillon de nuit (n) (m)
moth

pâquerette (n) (f)
daisy

parapluie (n) (m)
umbrella (for rain)

parasol (n) (m)
umbrella (for sun)

parc (n) (m)
park

parce que (conj)
because

parent (n) (m)
parent

paresseux/paresseuse (adj)
lazy

parfait/parfaite (adj)
perfect

particulier/particulière (adj)
special

partie (n) (f)
part

partout (adv)
everywhere

pas (n) (m)
step

passage clouté (n) (m)
zebra crossing

passager/passagère (n) (m/f)
passenger

passé (n) (m)
past (history)

passeport (n) (m)
passport

pastèque (n) (f)
watermelon

pâte à modeler (n) (f)
modelling clay

pâtes (n) (f)
pasta

patient/patiente (adj)
patient

patient/patiente (n) (m/f)
patient

patinage sur glace (n) (m)
ice skating

patte (n) (f)
foot (animal), paw

pause (n) (f)
break

pauvre (adj)
poor

pays (n) (m)
country

peau (n) (f)
skin

pêche (n) (f)
fishing

pédale (n) (f)
pedal

peigne (n) (m)
comb

peinture (n) (f)
paint

pélican (n) (m)
pelican

pelle (n) (f)
spade

pelouse (n) (f)
lawn

pendant (prep)
during

pendant que (conj)
while

père (n) (m)
father

perle (n) (f)
bead

perroquet (n) (m)
parrot

personne (pron)
nobody

personne (n) (f)
person

personne âgée (n) (f)
old person

petit/petite (adj)
little, small

petit ami (m)
boyfriend

petit-déjeuner (n) (m)
breakfast

petit pain (m)
(bread) roll

petit pois (m)
pea

petit tapis (m)
mat

petite amie (f)
girlfriend

peu profond/peu profonde (adj)
shallow

peut-être (adv)
maybe, perhaps

phare (n) (m)
lighthouse

pharmacie (n) (f)
chemist

phoque (n) (m)
seal

photo (n) (f)
photo

piano (n) (m)
piano

pièce (n) (f)
coin, room

pièce de théâtre (n) (f)
play

pied (n) (m)
foot

pierre (n) (f)
stone

pile (n) (f)
battery

pilote (n) (m)
pilot

pin (n) (m)
pine tree

pinceau (n) (m)
paint brush

pique-nique (n) (m)
picnic

pire (adj)
worst

piscine (n) (f)
swimming pool

pissenlit (n) (m)
dandelion

pizza (n) (f)
pizza

placard (n) (m)
cupboard

plafond (n) (m)
ceiling

plage (n) (f)
beach

planche de surf (n) (f)
surfboard

planète (n) (f)
planet

plante (n) (f)
plant

plat/plate (adj)
flat, level

plateau (n) (m)
tray

plein/pleine (adj)
full

plongée (n) (f)
diving

pluie (n) (f)
rain

plume (n) (f)
feather

plus que
more than

pneu (n) (m)
tyre

poche (n) (f)
pocket

poêle (n) (f)
frying pan

poils (n) (m)
fur

poilu/poilue (adj)
hairy

point (n) (m)
point

poire (n) (f)
pear

poisson (n) (m)
fish

poisson rouge (n) (m)
goldfish

poitrine (n) (f)
chest

poivre (n) (m)
pepper

polaire (n) (f)
fleece

police (n) (f)
police

pomme (n) (f)
apple

pomme de pin (n) (f)
pinecone

pomme de terre (n) (f)
potato

pompier (n) (m)
firefighter

pont (n) (m)
bridge, deck (boat)

populaire (adj)
popular

port (n) (m)
harbour

porte (n) (f)
door

porte d'entrée (n) (f)
front door

porte-monnaie (n) (m)
purse

possible (adj)
possible

poste (n) (f)
mail

pot de peinture (n) (m)
paint tin

poteau (n) (m)
pole

poubelle (n) (f)
bin

pouce (n) (m)
thumb

poudre (n) (f)
powder

poulet (n) (m)
chicken

poupée (n) (f)
doll

pourquoi (adv)
why

poussette (n) (f)
buggy

poussière (n) (f)
dust

poussin (n) (m)
chick

préféré/préférée (adj)
favourite

premier/première (adj)
first

premiers secours (n) (m)
first aid

près de (prep)
near

président/e (n) (m/f)
president

presque (adv)
almost, nearly

prêt/prête (adj)
ready

prince (n) (m)
prince

princesse (n) (f)
princess

principal/principale (adj)
main

printemps (n) (m)
spring (season)

prise électrique (n) (f)
plug (electric)

prix (n) (m)
price, prize

probablement (adv)
probably

problème (n) (m)
problem

prochain/prochaine (adj)
next

proche (adj)
close (near)

profond/profonde (adj)
deep

projet (n) (m)
project

promenade (n) (f)
walk

propre (adj)
clean, own

prudent/prudente (adj)
careful

pull (n) (m)
sweater

pull-over (n) (m)
jumper

punaise (n) (f)
drawing pin

puzzle (n) (m)
puzzle

pyjama (n) (m)
pyjamas

Q

quai (n) (m)
platform

quand (adv)
when

quart (n) (m)
quarter

quelque chose (pron)
something

quelquefois (adv)
sometimes

quelques (adj)
some

quelqu'un (pron)
someone

question (n) (f)
question

queue (n) (f)
queue, tail

qui (pron)
who

quiz (n) (m)
quiz

R

racine (n) (f)
root

radio (n) (f)
radio

raide (adj)
steep

raisin (n) (m)
grape

rame (n) (f)
oar

rapide (adj)
fast

raquette (n) (f)
racket

rat (n) (m)
rat

râteau (n) (m)
rake

rayures (n) (f)
stripes

recette (n) (f)
recipe

récolte (n) (f)
crop

récréation (n) (f)
playtime

rectangle (n) (m)
rectangle

réel/réelle (adj)
real

réfrigérateur (n) (m)
fridge

région (n) (f)
area

règle (n) (f)
ruler (measuring)

reine (n) (f)
queen

renard (n) (m)
fox

repas (n) (m)
meal

réponse (n) (f)
answer

requin (n) (m)
shark

restaurant (n) (m)
restaurant

rêve (n) (m)
dream

réveil (n) (m)
alarm clock

réverbère (n) (m)
street light

rhinocéros (n) (m)
rhinoceros

riche (adj)
rich

rideau (n) (m)
curtain

rien (pron)
nothing

rigolo (adj)
fun

rive (n) (f)
bank (river)

rivière (n) (f)
river

riz (n) (m)
rice

robe (n) (f)
dress

robinet (n) (m)
tap

robot (n) (m)
robot

rocher (n) (m)
rock

roi (n) (m)
king

rond/ronde (adj)
round

rose (adj)
pink

rose (n) (f)
rose

roue (n) (f)
wheel

rouge (adj)
red

route (n) (f)
road

ruban (n) (m)
ribbon

ruche (n) (f)
hive

rue (n) (f)
street

rugby (n) (m)
rugby

rugueux/rugueuse (adj)
rough

S

s'il te plaît
please

sable (n) (m)
sand

sac (n) (m)
bag, sack, shopping bag

sac à dos (n) (m)
backpack, rucksack

sac à main (n) (m)
handbag

sac de couchage (n) (m)
sleeping bag

sac en plastique (n) (m)
plastic bag

saison (n) (f)
season

salade (n) (f)
salad

salaire (n) (m)
pay

sale (adj)
dirty

salle à manger (n) (f)
dining room

salle de bains (n) (f)
bathroom

salle de classe (n) (f)
classroom

salon (n) (m)
living room

salut
hi

sandalette (n) (f)
sandal

sandwich (n) (m)
sandwich

sang (n) (m)
blood

sans (prep)
without

sauterelle (n) (f)
grasshopper

savon (n) (m)
soap

scarabée (n) (m)
beetle

sciences (n) (f)
science

scientifique (n) (m/f)
scientist

score (n) (m)
score

seau (n) (m)
bucket

sec/sèche (adj)
dry

secours (n) (m)
rescue

sel (n) (m)
salt

selle (n) (f)
saddle

semaine (n) (f)
week

sens (n) (m)
meaning

séparément (adv)
apart

serpent (n) (m)
snake

serre (n) (f)
greenhouse

serré/serrée (adj)
tight

serveuse (n) (f)
waitress

serviette (n) (f)
towel

serviette de toilette (n) (f)
flannel

seul/seule (adj)
alone

seulement (adv)
only

sévère (adj)
strict

shampooing (n) (m)
shampoo

short (n) (m)
shorts

sifflement (n) (m)
whistle

silencieux/silencieuse (adj)
quiet

singe (n) (m)
monkey

site web (n) (m)
website

skate-board (n) (m)
skateboard

ski (n) (m)
skiing

snowboard (n) (m)
snowboard

sœur (n) (f)
sister

soir (n) (m)
evening

sol (n) (m)
floor

soldat (n) (m)
soldier

soleil (n) (m)
sun

solide (n) (m)
solid

sombre (adj)
dark

son/sa (adj)
her / his / its

sorte (n) (f)
kind (type)

sortie (n) (f)
way out

sourcil (n) (m)
eyebrow

sourd/sourde (adj)
deaf

souris (n) (f)
mouse (animal, computer)

sous (prep)
under

sous-marin (n) (m)
submarine

sous-vêtements (n) (m)
underwear

souvenir (n) (m)
souvenir

souvent (adv)
often

spaghettis (n) (m)
spaghetti

spectacle (n) (m)
show

sport (n) (m)
sport

squelette (n) (m)
skeleton

stupide (adj)
stupid

stylo (n) (m)
pen

sucre (n) (m)
sugar

sud (n) (m)
south

sujet (n) (m)
subject

supermarché (n) (m)
supermarket

supplémentaire (adj)
extra

sur (prep)
about, on top of

sûr/sûre (adj)
sure

surf (n) (m)
surfing

surface (n) (f)
surface

surprise (n) (f)
surprise

surveillant de baignade (n) (m)
lifeguard

sympathique (adj)
nice

T

table (n) (f)
table

tableau (n) (m)
picture

tableau noir (n) (m)
blackboard

tablier (n) (m)
apron

taches (n) (f)
spots

taille (n) (f)
size, waist

tante (n) (f)
aunt

tapis (n) (m)
rug

tapis de souris (n) (m)
mouse mat

tasse (n) (m)
cup, mug

taxi (n) (m)
taxi

tee-shirt (n) (m)
T-shirt

télécommande (n) (f)
remote control

téléphone (n) (m)
phone (n)

téléphone portable (n) (m)
mobile phone

télescope (n) (m)
telescope

télévision (n) (f)
television

temps (n) (m)
weather

temps libre (n) (m)
free time

tennis (n) (m)
tennis

tennis de table (n) (m)
table tennis

tente (n) (f)
tent

terrain (n) (m)
land

Terre (n) (f)
Earth (planet)

terre (n) (f)
ground, soil

terrible (adj)
terrible

têtard (n) (m)
tadpole

tête (n) (f)
head

texto (n) (m)
text message

thé (n) (m)
tea

thermomètre (n) (m)
thermometer

ticket de caisse (n) (m)
receipt

tige (n) (f)
stem

tigre (n) (m)
tiger

timbre (n) (m)
stamp

timide (adj)
shy

tiroir (n) (m)
drawer

tissu (n) (m)
cloth

toilettes (n) (f)
toilet

toit (n) (m)
roof

tomate (n) (f)
tomato

tondeuse à gazon (n) (f)
lawn mower

torchon (n) (m)
tea towel

tornade (n) (f)
tornado

tortue (n) (f)
tortoise

tortue de mer (n) (f)
turtle

tôt (adv)
early

toucan (n) (m)
toucan

toujours (adv)
always

touriste (n) (m/f)
tourist

tournant (n) (m)
turn (bend)

tournesol (n) (m)
sunflower

tourniquet (n) (m)
roundabout

tous (adj)
every

tous les jours (adv)
everyday

tout (pron)
everything

tout/toute (adj)
all

tout à coup (adv)
suddenly

tout de suite (adv)
immediately

tout le monde (pron)
everybody

toux (n) (f)
cough

tracteur (n) (m)
tractor

train (n) (m)
train, train set

traîneau (n) (m)
sleigh

trajet (n) (m)
route

tranquille (adj)
peaceful

tranquillement (adv)
quietly

transport (n) (m)
transport

très (adv)
very

triangle (n) (m)
triangle

triste (adj)
sad

troisième (adj)
third

trombone (n) (m)
paper clip

trompe (n) (f)
trunk (animal)

tronc (n) (m)
trunk (tree)

tropical/tropicale (adj)
tropical

trottoir (n) (m)
pavement

trou (n) (m)
hole

troupeau (n) (m)
flock (of sheep)

trousse (n) (f)
pencil case

tu/vous (pron)
you

tube (n) (m)
tube

tunnel (n) (m)
tunnel

U

un/une (article)
a, an

uniforme (n) (m)
uniform

uniforme scolaire (n) (m)
school uniform

univers (n) (m)
universe

urgence (n) (f)
emergency

usine (n) (f)
factory

utile (adj)
useful

V

vacances (n) (f)
holiday

vache (n) (f)
cow

vague (n) (f)
wave

vaisselle (n) (f)
washing-up

valise (n) (f)
suitcase

veau (n) (m)
calf

vedette de cinéma (n) (f)
film star

végétarien/végétarienne (n) (m/f)
vegetarian

vélo (n) (m)
bike

vendeur/vendeuse (n) (m/f)
shop assistant

vent (n) (m)
wind

ventre (n) (m)
tummy

ver (n) (m)
worm

ver de terre (n) (m)
earthworm

verbe (n) (m)
verb

verre (n) (m)
glass (drink)

vers (prep)
towards

vert/verte (adj)
green

vêtements (n) (m)
clothes

vétérinaire (n) (m/f)
vet

viande (n) (f)
meat

vide (adj)
empty

vie (n) (f)
life

vieux/vieille (adj)
old

vilain/vilaine (adj)
naughty

village (n) (m)
village

ville (n) (f)
city, town

violet/violette (adj)
purple

violon (n) (m)
violin

visage (n) (m)
face

vite (adv)
quickly

voile (n) (f)
sail

voisin/voisine (n) (m/f)
neighbour

voiture (n) (f)
car

voiture de course (n) (f)
racing car

voiture de police (n) (f)
police car

votre (adj)
your

voyage (n) (m)
journey, trip

vrai/vraie (adj)
true

vraiment (adv)
really

V. T. T. (n) (m)
mountain bike

W

week-end (n) (m)
weekend

Y

yacht (n) (m)
yacht

yaourt (n) (m)
yoghurt

Z

zèbre (n) (m)
zebra

zone (n) (f)
zone

zoo (n) (m)
zoo

Speaking French

In this dictionary, we have spelled out each French word in a way that will help you pronounce it. Use this guide to help you understand how the word should sound when you say it. Some French words look the same as English, but sound very different!

Letter	Pronunciation	Our spelling	Example
a, à, â	between the *a* in h*a*t and f*a*r	*a* or *ah*	**adresse** *a-dreys*
ch	like *sh* in *sh*ip	*sh*	**changer** *shahn-zhay*
ç	like *s* in *s*it	*s*	**garçon** *gar-so(n)*
é	like *ay* in d*ay*	*ay*	**café** *ka-fay*
è, ê	like *e* in m*e*t	*eh*	**crème** *krehm*
e	like *er* in oth*er*	*uh*	**de** *duh*
gn	like the *ni* in o*ni*on	*nye*	**ligne** *leen-ye*
i, y	like *ee* in f*ee*t	*ee*	**fille** *fee-ye*
j, and sometimes g	like *s* in mea*s*ure	*zh*	**bonjour** *bon-zhoor*
qu	like *k* in *k*ing	*k*	**queue** *kuh*
o, ô	like *o* in m*o*re	*o* or *oh*	**porte** *port*
r	say *ruh* at the back of your throat, as if you're gargling	*r*	**fleur** *fluhr*
u	like *ew* in f*ew*	*ew*	**tu** *tew*
an, en, ien, in, ain, ein, on, un am, em, im, aim, eim, om, um	the *n* is not pronounced, but the vowel in front of it should have a nasal sound, as if the word ended in *ng*. For example, as if you said *song*, but stopped before saying the final *ng*.	*a(n), ah(n), o(n)*	**bien** *bya(n)*

113

A B C D E F G H I J K L M N O P Q R S T U V W X Y Z

Verbs

This section gives a list of useful verbs (doing words). You have the infinitive (to...) of the verb. The most useful verbs, such as "to be" *être* and "to have" *avoir*, are written out so that you can see how they change depending on who is doing the action. I = je, you = tu, he/she = il/elle, we = nous, you (plural and formal) = vous and they = ils/elles.

We have also written out three of the most regular French verbs: to give = *donner*, to finish = *finir* and to sell = *vendre*, so you can see how these change.

There is also a reflexive verb written out. Reflexive verbs are often used where you would say "myself" or "yourself" in English. An example is: to wash oneself = *se laver*.

The verbs that are written out are shown in the present tense – they describe what is happening now.

to act
faire du théâtre
fair dew tay-a-truh

to agree
être d'accord
eh-truh da-kor

to allow
permettre
pair-met-truh

to appear
apparaître
ap-par-eh-truh

to ask
demander
duh-mahn-day

to bake
faire de la pâtisserie
fair duh la paht-eess-ree

to bark
aboyer
ab-wa-yay

to be
être
eh-truh

I am
je suis
you are
tu es
he, she is
il, elle est
we are
nous sommes
you (plural) are
vous êtes
they are
ils, elles sont

to be able
pouvoir
poov-wahr

to be born
être né
eh-truh nay

to be called
être appelé
eh-truh ap-play

to be cold
avoir froid
av-wahr frwa

to be hungry
avoir faim
av-wahr fa(m)

to be scared of
avoir peur de
av-wahr puhr duh

to be thirsty
avoir soif
av-wahr swaf

to become
devenir
duh-vuh-neer

Je fais de la pâtisserie.

Simon croque une pomme.

Elle gonfle un ballon.

Louise **porte** les sacs.

to begin
commencer
kom-ahn-say

to behave
se comporter
suh kom-por-tay

to believe
croire
krwahr

to bend
plier
plee-yay

to bird-watch
observer les oiseaux
ob-zair-vay layz wa-zoh

to bite
croquer
kro-kay

to block
bloquer
blo-kay

to blow
gonfler
gon-flay

to boil
bouillir
boo-yeer

to borrow
emprunter
ahm-pran-tay

to bounce
rebondir
ruh-bon-deer

to brake
freiner
fray-nay

to break
casser
kah-say

to breathe
respirer
ruh-speer-ay

to bring
apporter
ap-por-tay

to brush
brosser
bros-say

to brush one's teeth
se brosser les dents
suh bros-say lay dah(n)

to build
construire
kon-strweer

to bump into
rentrer dans
rahn-tray dah(n)

to buy
acheter
ash-tay

to camp
camper
kahm-pay

to carry
porter
por-tay

to catch
attraper
at-tra-pay

to cause
causer
koh-zay

to celebrate
célébrer
say-lay-bray

to change
changer
shahn-zhay

to charge (a phone)
recharger
ruh-shar-zhay

to check
vérifier
vair-eef-yay

to choose
choisir
shwa-zeer

to clean
nettoyer
net-wa-yay

to clear (a table)
débarrasser
day-bar-ra-say

to climb
grimper
gram-pay

to close
fermer
fair-may

Attrape le ballon !

A B C D E F G H I J K L M N O P Q R S T U V W X Y Z

115

A B C D E F G H I J K L M N O P Q R S T U V W X Y Z

to collect
collectionner
kol-lek-syo-nay

to come
venir
vuh-neer

to come back
revenir
ruh-vuh-neer

to come from
venir de
vuh-neer duh

to compare
comparer
kom-pa-ray

to complain
se plaindre
suh plan-druh

to contain
contenir
kon-tuh-neer

to continue
continuer
kon-teen-ew-ay

to cook
cuisiner
kwee-zee-nay

to copy
copier
kop-yay

to cost
coûter
koo-tay

to count
compter
kom-tay

to cover
couvrir
koov-reer

to crack
casser
kass-say

to crash
s'écraser
say-krah-zay

to create
créer
kray-ay

to cross
traverser
tra-vair-say

to cry
pleurer
pluhr-ay

to cut
couper
koo-pay

to cut out
découper
day-koo-pay

to cycle
faire du vélo
fair dew vay-lo

to dance
danser
dahn-say

to decide
décider
day-see-day

to decorate
décorer
day-ko-ray

to describe
décrire
day-kreer

to destroy
détruire
day-trweer

to die
mourir
moo-reer

to dig
creuser
kruh-zay

Marie danse bien.

Caroline creuse dans le sable.

Stéphane jardine.

to disappear
disparaître
dees-par-eh-truh

to discover
découvrir
day-koov-reer

to dive
plonger
plon-jay

to do
faire
fair

I do
je fais
you do
tu fais
he/she does
il/elle fait
we do
nous faisons
you (plural) do
vous faites
they do
ils/elles font

to do the gardening
jardiner
zhar-dee-nay

to draw
dessiner
dess-ee-nay

to dream
rêver
reh-vay

to dress up
s'habiller
sa-bee-yay

to drink
boire
bwahr

to drive
conduire
kon-dweer

to dry
sécher
say-shay

to earn
gagner
gan-yay

to eat
manger
mahn-zhay

to encourage
encourager
ahn-koo-ra-zhay

to enjoy
aimer
eh-may

to escape
s'échapper
say-shap-pay

to explain
expliquer
eks-plee-kay

to explode
exploser
ek-sploh-zay

to face
affronter
af-fron-tay

to fall
tomber
tom-bay

to fall down
s'écrouler
say-kroo-lay

to feed
nourrir
noo-reer

to feel
ressentir
ruh-sahn-teer

to fetch
aller chercher
al-lay shair-shay

to fight
se battre
suh bat-truh

to fill
remplir
rahm-pleer

to find
trouver
troo-vay

to find out
se renseigner sur
suh rahn-sen-yay soor

*Je **mange** un gâteau au chocolat.*

*Il faut **nourrir** les chiens !*

A B C D E F G H I J K L M N O P Q R S T U V W X Y Z

117

A B C D E F G H I J K L M N O P Q R S T U V W X Y Z

to finish
finir
feen-eer

I finish
je finis
you finish
tu finis
he/she finishes
il/elle finit
we finish
nous finissons
you finish
vous finissez
they finish
ils/elles finissent

to float
flotter
flot-tay

to fly
voler
vo-lay

to fold
plier
plee-yay

to follow
suivre
sweev-ruh

to forget
oublier
oo-blee-yay

to freeze
geler
zhuh-lay

to frighten
effrayer
eh-fray-yay

Plie le papier.

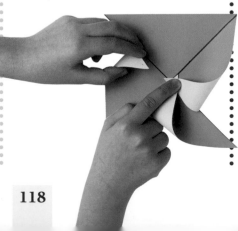

to get
recevoir
ruh-suhv-wahr

to get on (a bus)
monter
mon-tay

to get ready
se préparer
suh pray-pa-ray

to get up
se lever
suh le-vay

to give
donner
don-nay

I give
je donne
you give
tu donnes
he/she gives
il/elle donne
we give
nous donnons
you (plural) give
vous donnez
they give
ils/elles donnent

to go
aller
ah-lay

I go
je vais
you go
tu vas
he/she goes
il/elle va
we go
nous allons
you (plural) go
vous allez
they go
ils/elles vont

to go camping
faire du camping
fair dew kahm-peeng

to go on holiday
partir en vacances
par-teer ah(n) vak-ahns

to go out
sortir
sor-teer

to go shopping
faire les courses
fair lay koorss

to grow
pousser
poo-say

to guess
deviner
duh-vee-nay

to hang up (a phone)
raccrocher
rak-ro-shay

to happen
arriver
ar-ree-vay

to hate
détester
day-tes-tay

Bruno prend des œufs pour le petit-déjeuner.

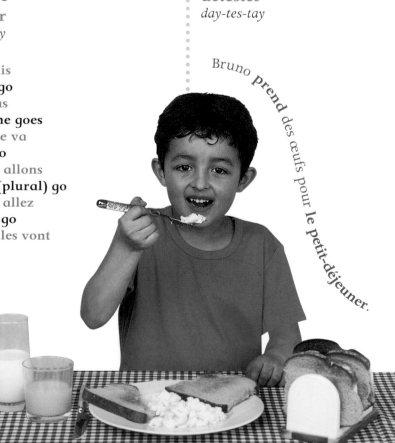

118

Sophie *s'amuse* !

to have
avoir
av-wahr
I have
j'ai
you have
tu as
he/she has
il/elle a
we have
nous avons
you (plural) have
vous avez
they have
ils/elles ont

to have a shower
prendre une douche
prahn-druh ewn doosh

to have breakfast
prendre le petit-déjeuner
prahn-druh luh puh-tee day-zhuh-nay

to have fun
s'amuser
sam-ew-zay

to have to
devoir
duhv-wahr

to hear
entendre
ahn-tahn-druh

to help
aider
eh-day

to hide
cacher
ka-shay

to hit
frapper
frap-pay

to hold
tenir
tuh-neer

to hop
sauter
soh-tay

to hope
espérer
es-pair-ay

to hurry
se dépêcher
suh day-peh-shay

to hurt
blesser
bless-ay

to imagine
imaginer
ee-ma-zhee-nay

to include
inclure
an-klewr

to inspire
inspirer
an-spee-ray

to invent
inventer
an-vahn-tay

to invite
inviter
an-vee-tay

to join
joindre
zhwan-druh

to jump
sauter
soh-tay

to keep
garder
gar-day

to kick
donner un coup de pied
don-nay a(n) koo duh pyay

to kill
tuer
tew-ay

to kiss
embrasser
ahm-bra-say

to know (someone)
connaître
kon-neh-truh

to know (something)
savoir
sav-wahr

Les grenouilles **sautent** haut.

A B C D E F G H I J K L M N O P Q R S T U V W X Y Z

119

to land (in a plane)
atterrir
at-tair-eer

to last
durer
dew-ray

to laugh
rire
reer

to lay a table
mettre la table
met-truh la tab-luh

to leap
bondir
bon-deer

to learn
apprendre
ap-prahn-druh

to lie
mentir
mahn-teer

to lift
lever
luh-vay

to like
aimer
eh-may

to listen to
écouter
ay-koo-tay

to live
vivre
veev-ruh

to lock
fermer à clé
fair-may ah klay

to look
regarder
ruh-gar-day

to look after
s'occuper de
sok-ew-pay duh

to look for
chercher
shair-shay

to lose
perdre
pair-druh

to love
adorer
ad-or-ay

to magnify
grossir
groh-seer

to make
fabriquer
fab-ree-kay

to make a wish
faire un vœu
fair a(n) vuh

to make friends
se faire des amis
suh fair dez a-mee

to marry
se marier
suh mar-yay

to mean
signifier
seen-yeef-yay

to meet
rencontrer
rahn-kon-tray

to move
bouger
boo-zhay

to need
avoir besoin de
av-wahr buh-zwah(n) duh

to not feel well
ne pas se sentir bien
nuh pah suh sahn-teer bya(n)

to notice
remarquer
ruh-mar-kay

to offer
offrir
off-reer

to open
ouvrir
oov-reer

Lucie **ouvre** la porte.

Philippe **écoute** de la musique.

Charlotte **regarde** de la terre.

to own
posséder
po-say-day

to pack
faire les valises
fair lay val-eez

to paint
peindre
pan-druh

to pay
payer
pay-yay

to persuade
persuader
pair-swa-day

to pick up
ramasser
ram-ah-say

to plan
organiser
or-gan-ee-zay

to play
jouer
zhoo-ay

to play an instrument
jouer d'un instrument
zhoo-ay dan an-strew-mah(n)

to point
indiquer
an-dee-kay

to pour
verser
vair-say

to practise
s'entraîner
sahn-treh-nay

to predict
prédire
pray-deer

to prefer
préférer
pray-fair-ay

to prepare
préparer
pray-pa-ray

to press
appuyer sur
ap-pwee-yay soor

to pretend
faire semblant
fair sahm-blah(n)

to print
imprimer
am-pree-may

to produce
produire
pro-dweer

to promise
promettre
pro-met-truh

to protect
protéger
pro-tay-zhay

to provide
fournir
foor-neer

to pull
tirer
teer-ay

to push
pousser
poo-say

to put
mettre
met-truh

to put away
ranger
rahn-zhay

to rain
pleuvoir
pluhv-wahr

Verse l'eau doucement !

Peux-tu peindre un tableau ?

A B C D E F G H I J K L M N O P Q R S T U V W X Y Z

A B C D E F G H I J K L M N O P Q R S T U V W X Y Z

to reach
atteindre
at-tan-druh

to read
lire
leer

to realise
se rendre compte
suh rahn-druh komt

to recognise
reconnaître
ruh-kon-neh-truh

to refuse
refuser
ruh-few-zay

to relax
se détendre
suh day-tahn-druh

to remain
rester
res-tay

to remember
se souvenir de
suh soo-vuh-neer duh

to repair
réparer
ray-pa-ray

to rest
se reposer
suh ruh-poh-zay

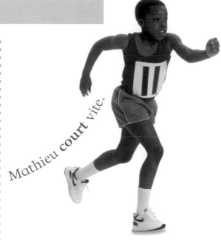

Mathieu **court** vite.

to return
revenir
ruh-vuh-neer

to ride a bike
faire du vélo
fair dew vay-lo

to ride a horse
monter à cheval
mon-tay ah shuh-val

to ring
sonner
so-nay

to roll
rouler
roo-lay

to row
se promener en barque
suh pro-muh-nay ah(n) bark

to rub
frotter
fro-tay

to run
courir
koo-reer

to run after
poursuivre
poor-swee-vruh

to sail
faire de la voile
fair duh la vwal

to save
sauver
soh-vay

to say
dire
deer

to score (a goal)
marquer
mar-kay

to scratch (oneself)
se gratter
suh grat-tay

to search
chercher
shair-shay

to see
voir
vwahr

to seem
sembler
sahm-blay

Julie **lit** son livre.

Mélanie **monte** à cheval.

to sell
vendre
vahn-druh

I sell
je vends
you sell
tu vends
he/she sells
il/elle vend
we sell
nous vendons
you (plural) sell
vous vendez
they sell
ils/elles vendent

to send
envoyer
ahn-vwa-yay

to share
partager
par-ta-zhay

to shine
briller
bree-yay

to shout
crier
kree-yay

to show
montrer
mon-tray

Clément dort.

to sing
chanter
shahn-tay

to sit
s'asseoir
sass-wahr

to skate (on ice)
patiner (sur glace)
pa-tee-nay

to skate (roller)
faire du roller
fair dew ro-lair

to ski
skier
skee-yay

to sleep
dormir
dor-meer

to slide
glisser
glee-say

to slip
glisser
glee-say

to smell
sentir
sahn-teer

to smile
sourire
soo-reer

to snow
neiger
nay-zhay

Léa **crie** après son amie.

to sound (like)
sembler
sahm-blay

to speak
parler
par-lay

to spell
épeler
ay-puh-lay

to spin
tourner
toor-nay

to spread
étaler
ay-ta-lay

to stand
se tenir debout
suh tuh-neer duh-boo

to stand up
se lever
suh luh-vay

to start
commencer
kom-ahn-say

to stay
rester
res-tay

to stick
coller
kol-lay

Étale le chocolat sur les gâteaux.

A B C D E F G H I J K L M N O P Q R S T U V W X Y Z

A B C D E F G H I J K L M N O P Q R S T U V W X Y Z

La fille prend une photo.

to sting
piquer
pee-kay

to stop
arrêter
arh-reh-tay

to stretch
s'étirer
say-teer-ay

to study
étudier
ay-tewd-yay

to surf
surfer
soor-fay

to surprise
surprendre
soor-prahn-druh

to survive
survivre
soor-veev-ruh

to swim
nager
na-zhay

to take
prendre
prahn-druh

to take a photo
prendre une photo
prahn-druh ewn fo-toh

to take away
emporter
ahm-por-tay

to take turns
faire à tour de rôle
fair ah toor duh rohl

to talk
parler
par-lay

to taste
goûter
goo-tay

to teach
enseigner
ahn-sen-yay

to tease
taquiner
tak-ee-nay

to tell
raconter
rak-on-tay

to tell a story
raconter une histoire
rak-on-tay ewn eest-wahr

to tell the time
dire l'heure
deer luhr

to thank
remercier
ruh-mair-syay

to think
réfléchir
ray-flay-sheer

Valérie réfléchit.

to throw
jeter
zhuh-tay

to tidy up
ranger
rahn-zhay

to tie
attacher
at-ta-shay

to touch
toucher
too-shay

to train
entraîner
ahn-treh-nay

to translate
traduire
trad-weer

to travel
voyager
vwa-ya-zhay

to treat (well)
traiter (bien)
tray-tay bya(n)

to try (on)
essayer
es-say-yay

to turn
tourner
toor-nay

Jean s'entraîne.

to type
taper
ta-pay

to understand
comprendre
kom-prahn-druh

to undress
se déshabiller
suh day-sa-bee-yay

to unpack
déballer
day-bal-lay

to use
utiliser
ew-tee-lee-zay

to visit
visiter
vee-zee-tay

to wait
attendre
at-tahn-druh

to wake up
se réveiller
suh ray-vay-yay

to walk
marcher
mar-shay

*Pierre **tape** sur son clavier.*

*Manon **lave** la vaisselle.*

to want
vouloir
vool-wahr

to warm
réchauffer
ray-shoh-fay

to wash
laver
la-vay

to wash (oneself)
se laver
suh la-vay

I wash
je me lave
you wash
tu te laves
he/she washes
il/elle se lave
we wash
nous nous lavons
you (plural) wash
vous vous lavez
they wash
ils/elles se lavent

to wash the dishes
laver la vaisselle
la-vay la vay-sel

to watch
regarder
ruh-gar-day

to wave
faire un signe de la main
fair a(n) seen-ye duh la ma(n)

to wear
porter
por-tay

to weigh
peser
puh-zay

to whisper
chuchoter
shew-sho-tay

to win
gagner
gan-yay

to wish
souhaiter
sway-tay

to wonder
se demander
suh duh-mahn-day

to work
travailler
tra-va-yay

to work (function)
fonctionner
fonk-syo-nay

to wrap
emballer
ahm-bal-lay

to write
écrire
ay-kreer

*Julien **écrit** dans son journal.*

A
B
C
D
E
F
G
H
I
J
K
L
M
N
O
P
Q
R
S
T
U
V
W
X
Y
Z

Useful phrases
Expressions utiles

Yes
Oui
wee

No
Non
no(n)

Hello
Bonjour
bon-zhoor

Goodbye
Au revoir
oh ruhv-wahr

See you later
À bientôt
ah byan-toh

Please
S'il te plaît
seel tuh pleh

Thank you
Merci
mair-see

Excuse me
Excuse-moi
eks-kewz mwa

I'm sorry
Je suis désolé
zhuh swee day-zo-lay

My name is…
Je m'appelle…
zhuh ma-pel

I live…
J'habite à…
zha-beet ah

I am… years old.
J'ai… ans.
zhay…ah(n)

I don't understand
Je ne comprends pas
zhuh nuh
kom-prah(n) pah

I don't know
Je ne sais pas
zhuh nuh say pah

Very well
Très bien
treh bya(n)

> *Learn the days of the week*

Monday
lundi
lahn-dee

Tuesday
mardi
mar-dee

Wednesday
mercredi
mair-kruh-dee

Thursday
jeudi
zhuh-dee

Friday
vendredi
vahn-druh-dee

Saturday
samedi
sam-dee

Sunday
dimanche
dee-mahnsh

Very much
Beaucoup
boh-koo

I like/I don't like
J'aime/Je n'aime pas…
zhehm/zhuh nehm pah

Let's go!
Allons-y !
alohn-zee

Happy Birthday!
Bon anniversaire !
bo(n) an-ee-vair-sair

> *Bonjour, je m'appelle Luc.*

How are you?
Comment ça va ?
ko-mah(n) sa va

What is your name?
Comment t'appelles-tu ?
ko-mah(n) ta-pel tew

Do you speak…?
Parles-tu… ?
parl tew

Do you like…?
Aimes-tu… ?
ehm tew

Do you have…?
As-tu… ?
ah tew

Can I have…?
Puis-je avoir… ?
pwee zhuh av-wahr

How much…?
Combien… ?
kom-bya(n)

What's that?
Qu'est-ce que c'est ?
kess kuh say

How many?
Combien ?
kom-bya(n)

Can you help me?
Peux-tu m'aider ?
puh tew meh-day

What time is it?
Quelle heure est-il ?
kel uhr et eel

Help!
Au secours !
oh suh-koor

Stop!
Arrête !
ar-reht

Turn right/left
Tourne à droite/à gauche
toorn ah drwat/ah gohsh

Go straight on
Va tout droit
va too drwa

In front of
Devant
duh-vah(n)

Next to
À côté de
ah koh-tay duh

Where is/are…?
Où est/sont… ?
oo eh/so(n)

Learn the months of the year

January
janvier
zhahnv-yay

February
février
fay-vree-yay

March
mars
mars

April
avril
av-reel

May
mai
may

June
juin
zhwa(n)

July
juillet
zhwee-yay

August
août
oot

September
septembre
sep-tahm-bruh

October
octobre
ok-to-bruh

November
novembre
no-vahm-bruh

December
décembre
day-sahm-bruh

Allons-y !

Useful phrases

Les nombres

Numbers

0 zéro
zay-roh
zero

1 un
a(n)
one

2 deux
duh
two

3 trois
trwa
three

4 quatre
kat-ruh
four

5 cinq
sank
five

6 six
seess
six

7 sept
set
seven

8 huit
weet
eight

9 neuf
nuhf
nine

10 dix
deess
ten

11 onze
onz
eleven

12 douze
dooz
twelve

13 treize
trez
thirteen

14 quatorze
kat-orz
fourteen

15 quinze
kanz
fifteen

16 seize
sez
sixteen

17 dix-sept
dees-set
seventeen

18 dix-huit
deez-weet
eighteen

19 dix-neuf
dees-nuhf
nineteen

20 vingt
va(n)
twenty

21 vingt et un
vant ay a(n)
twenty-one

30 trente
trahnt
thirty

40 quarante
kar-ahnt
forty

50 cinquante
sank-ahnt
fifty

60 soixante
swa-sahnt
sixty

70 soixante-dix
swa-sahnt-dees
seventy

80 quatre-vingt
kat-ruh-va(n)
eighty

90 quatre-vingt-dix
kat-ruh-va(n)-deess
ninety

100 cent
sah(n)
hundred

Acknowledgements

DK would like to thank the following people:
Sarah Ponder and Carole Oliver for design help;
Marie Greenwood and Jennie Morris for editorial
help; Angela Wilkes for language consultancy;
Katherine Northam for digital artwork; Rose
Horridge for picture research; Rachael Swann
for picture research assistance; and
Hope Annets, Mary Mead, Bethany Tombs,

Todd and Sophie Yonwin for modelling.
The publisher would like to thank the
following for their kind permission to reproduce
their photographs: (Key: t = top, b = bottom,
r = right, l = left, c = centre)
31: www.aviationpictures.com/Austin J. Brown
1983 (tl); 31: Courtesy of FSTOP Pte. Ltd.,
Singapore (tc); 54: Corbis/Ronnie Kaufman (br);
55: Corbis/Craig Tuttle (tl); 55: Corbis/Craig
Tuttle (tr); 55: Zefa/J. Jaemsen (cl); 55: Zefa/J.

Jaemsen (cr); 55: Powerstock (bl); 72: Getty
Images/Stone/Stuart Westmorland (tl); 82:
Indianapolis Motor Speedway Foundation,
Inc. (tc); 91: David Edge (tc); 91: Courtesy of
Junior Department, Royal College of Music,
London (br).
All other images © Dorling Kindersley.
For further information see
www.dkimages.com